GET PAID!

5 STEPS TO GETTING YOUR INVOICES
PAID ON TIME, EVERY TIME

JAN REEVES

PRAISE FOR JAN REEVES

'Jan's company had some of the best quality systems I have ever seen. She is a strong, yet highly personable business leader who is well suited to growing successful businesses.'

Tony Hall, Managing Director, Navigator Consulting

'Jan headed up an exceptional business at Credit Recruitment. Her passion and knowledge of her industry meant that the relationships she built in the market over the years were impenetrable.'

Susie Hingston, Managing Director at The Loxley Group

'I've known Jan since 2003 and hold her in the highest regard. She is incredibly committed, professional and passionate. I seek her opinion as the person in business who I respect the most. Her feed-back, advice and wisdom are of great value to me.'

John Ratcliffe, Principle and Owner at Match Business Sales

PRAISE FOR *GET PAID!*

'With her book *GET PAID!* Jan has "hit the nail on the head". Lack of cashflow causes small business owners serious stress, stifles growth and annihilates profits. Not enough cash leads to business failure and worse.

'Getting invoices paid is not "rocket science" (as a lot of people seem to think) it's 99% admin and customer service and of course, Jan should know! Step by step she takes the cash-strapped business owner through the simple process of getting invoices paid easily and painlessly AND with the added benefit of improving relationships with customers.

'Literally, *GET PAID!* is the super-game-changer that small business has been waiting for.'

Tony Hall, Recruitment Industry Management Consultant, CEO, Senior Talent Specialist, Travel Industry Advisor and Board Member

'I am on the Board of 12 SME businesses and advise many others. Without a doubt, one of the most significant barriers to growth, and threats to sustainability, is cashflow management.

'This book should be compulsory reading for all business owners. It covers the full spectrum. Training customers, using technology, collection tactics, controlling the process and early warning signs, are just the beginning of what you will learn here.

'It's easy to follow, makes perfect sense and contains a litany of practical advice.

'Well done Jan. Business needs this book!'

Greg Savage, Recruitment Business Growth: Board Advisory, Consulting, Investment, Keynote Speaker

'Someone once said that getting paid in business is "not rocket science". It's not, but what it requires is a genuine empathy with your customer and an attitude that is fair but firm. This is your money after all, you are not a bank, or a lender and customers do need to understand and appreciate that right from the start.

'Jan's book is ideal for the small business owner that wants to enjoy a healthy profitable relationship with customers without the stress of lack of cash flow. Written in an easy manner and full of practical tips, this guide shows how you can get paid and enjoy your business and your customers.'

Terry Ledlin, LLB Notary Public, Special Counsel, Ledlin Lawyers

'Since implementing the first step of *GET PAID!* we have better control of our cashflow and can concentrate on growing the business rather than being distracted chasing payments. We now have strong repeatable systems and better controls thanks to *GET PAID!* Some small tweaks have made a big difference. Thank you, Jan!'

Sharon Austin, Director, Intelligent Recruitment

'Jan Reeves really knows this stuff. At one of our conferences she shared three tips with my GM that we immediately applied and brought in close to $50k in the following week. I'm so glad this book now exists to help other entrepreneurs achieve their mission and *GET PAID!*'

Glen Carlson, Director, Dent Global

'I found *GET PAID!* such an easy and succinct read – it's just brilliant information – I seriously enjoyed it!

'The biggest take home was how I can actually get paid AND improve and strengthen our customer relationships. The real-life scripts are also very helpful, and I can easily adapt these into our processes. Can't wait to put this knowledge into practice!'

Melissa Robson, Director, Divine Creative Agency

'Every single small business owner will face cash flow challenges at some stage, it simply goes with the territory. So much time and energy can be lost chasing money and worrying about money, making it a major issue.

'At long last someone has written a fantastic book designed to help small business owners to get paid. Congratulations to you Jan Reeves for writing the one book that every single small business owner needs to have by their side. I wish I had *GET PAID!* 35 years ago.'

Andrew Griffiths, International Bestselling Business Author, Commentator and Global Speaker

'If you are a small business owner with seriously overdue debtors and worried about your cash flow, the way I was – I couldn't even pay myself a wage – Jan's *GET PAID!* strategies are a life-saver. Just by implementing a few of Jan's simple tips I now have all my invoices paid on time, excellent relationships with my customers and a simple system to ensure my invoices are correct to save myself time. This book really is life changing and saves your business.'

Emma Small B.App.Sc(OT), Director Occupational Services Pty Ltd

'I got some really valuable insights from Jan's book – like making personal calls before invoicing: GOLD!'

Rico Soto, Founder/Director Fire Entertainment

'Making a sale is fantastic, but it's not really a sale until you see the money back in your bank. So how do you get paid, while preserving your customer relationships and maximising your revenue? There's no magic wand – the answer is systems.

'*GET PAID!* shows you in clear language, useful tips, and real-life experiences how to set up simple systems, already proven to get invoices paid. Through the five steps, you'll learn the best ways set up your AR and invoice process, through to the best way to ask for payment and everything else in between. And for customers who simply won't pay – how to successfully partner with third parties such as collections agencies.

'So, what's stopping you from getting paid?'

Dale Hannan MICM CCE, Managing Director & Katheryn Kershaw MICM, Client Services Director, National Collection Services

'I've been working with small business owners for nearly 20 years in our consulting practice. And I've surveyed more than 10,000 business owners too. There is no doubt that handling money is one of the biggest challenges for business owners, and one of the prime reasons why businesses fail.

'I highly recommend this book and Jan to you. The book contains an amazing amount of detailed advice that you can implement in your business to improve your cashflow and your client relationships too.'

Hunter Leonard, Author of Generation Experience *and Founder of Silver & Wise*

'GET PAID! is such a simple read, so practical and written in a format that anyone can understand and benefit from. I have to say that any business that offers credit to their customers would benefit from this book. SMEs who may only issue a small number of invoices each month would learn things that they never knew about. Well experienced credit providers could also benefit as we all fall into bad habits and brushing up on our practices is a necessity and should be part of an annual process review! P.S. I'm sending this book to my credit team.'

Colin Porter, Chief Executive Officer – CreditorWatch

'Jan's book *GET PAID!* is well written and easy to follow. It's well laid out and has very sound, easy-to-follow advice especially suitable to help the small business owner get paid.

'I've passed it to some new members of my team and their feedback is very positive, commenting on how it "joined a lot of dots" for them. The book put many things into context for them and gave them some very helpful tips to adopt.'

Arthur Tchetchenian, National Credit Manager, Transurban

'Jan's book is a super-easy read and contains a huge amount of valuable, practical information that you won't find readily available unless you've had the experience yourself.

'Using her expert knowledge and experience in this area she has set out a proven, easy-to-follow regime to get invoices paid and get paid on time. Highlighting "Key Points" and "To Do" suggestions at the end of each chapter practically does the work for you.'

Elizabeth McMurray, Teacher of Communication Success Strategies, Author of Power to Participate: How to mix and mingle with ease

THIS BOOK IS DEDICATED TO

Norman May,
who taught me that
'people pay people, and people pay people they like'

and

The staff, credit and collections professionals, and
clients of CRS who shared my vision and helped me
build a successful, award-winning service business

ACKNOWLEDGEMENTS

Thank you to …

Alek, who supports everything I do and has
always said I should write a book

Andrew Griffiths, who showed me it was possible

Aideen Gallagher, who cheered me on

Carole Harries, whose timely comment prompted me to finish

My editor Michael Hanrahan, who turned
it into something readable

Your customer can't pay you because they haven't been paid?

Gift a copy of this book to your customer to help them get paid – so they can pay you sooner. Order online or contact Jan at jan@janreeves.com for large orders.

First published in 2018 by Jan Reeves
https://janreeves.com/

A catalogue entry for this book is available from the National Library of Australia.

ISBN: 978-0-6484023-7-4

Project management and text design by Michael Hanrahan Publishing
Cover design by Peter Reardon

Disclaimer

CONTENTS

STEP 2: HOW TO FEEL 100% CONFIDENT ASKING FOR PAYMENT

STEP 3: THE 'INSIDER SECRET' AND HOW TO MINIMISE PROBLEMS THAT CAUSE PAYMENT DELAYS

Contents

STEP 5: RED FLAGS! HOW TO SPOT ONE AND WHAT TO DO ABOUT IT

FOREWORD

by Stephen Vaughan
Registered Liquidator and Licensed Commercial Agent
Certified Credit Executive, Australian Institute of Credit Management
Fellow, Australian Restructuring Insolvency & Turnaround Association
https://www.linkedin.com/in/stephenvaughan1

It's tough being in small business. There's no doubt about it. You've made the sale but your customer isn't paying. It doesn't seem fair. But whether you are a small or large business, a sale is not really a sale until the cash hits your bank account.

When you supply on credit, your valued customer becomes your 'debtor'. There are two types of debtors: those that won't pay and those that just can't. Fortunately, mostly it's a case of won't. Why is that? Well, there are usually very good reasons and, as this book will explain, excellent customer service doesn't end with the sale.

Whether I'm dealing with a metal fabricator, a clothing whole-saler, a labour hire company or even an accountant or a law firm, I see time and time again long-dated debts that have been left to fester or, worse, become uncollectable and then written off. This doesn't help you and, arguably, it doesn't help a good customer.

Don't underestimate this book because it's easy to read. *GET PAID!* takes a 'back to basics' approach. Some things may sound simple when you read them but you would be amazed how many businesses overlook these fundamentals, and suffer as a result. Don't be one of them.

There is much more to the art of getting paid than contracts, legal rights, debt collectors and going to court. I've been to court so many times I've lost count. When things have got to this point there are usually no winners.

Getting paid really is an art that you can learn and it's not rocket science! Helping your customer meet their commitments, pay you on time and buy from you again makes good sense. And, believe me, your customers will respect you all the more for it.

The five steps to getting paid set out in the following pages focus on the tools you will need, how to improve your confidence, 'training' your customers and dealing with barriers to being paid on time.

Remember I mentioned some customers can't pay? Or at least, they decided to pay someone else before you. Jan also explains the red flags to look for and what to do about it when you have a bad debt.

For 30 years I've been collecting debts, turning around under-performing businesses and liquidating those that fail. I've known Jan Reeves for over 25 of those years and shared in her passion for credit management because I know how essential it is to surviving in business. *GET PAID!* is not another dry and boring credit manual. It's about good business hygiene and getting into the mind of your customer.

Jan has somehow managed to distil a career's worth of real-life collections experience and the essentials to getting paid into this easy-to-read, insightful and impactful book. She even explains how to motive your team, increase their sense of satisfaction and, just perhaps, make it fun.

I thoroughly enjoyed reading this book and recommend it, whether you are a business person or even a seasoned credit professional.

This is a 'must read' for every small business that wants to improve cashflow, weatherproof your business and enhance your customer relationships.

INTRODUCTION

BUSTING COMMON PAYMENT MYTHS AND MISTAKES

'More than half of business owners worry about cashflow every month and just about all of them have unpaid invoices that could relieve the pressure.'

Colin Porter, Founder & Managing Director, CreditorWatch

Lots of business owners think that other businesses don't pay invoices just because they want to hold on to their money. After over 40 years of working with unpaid invoices, I can tell you categorically that this is *not* true. In my experience most invoices aren't paid on time because there's something missing in the sales process. (Read more about this on page 44.)

Whereas most books on the subject of getting paid are technical and treat 'collections' or 'getting paid' as an operation that happens only *after* a customer hasn't paid, by incorporating 'getting paid' into the sales process, and with a few tweaks to your admin processes, you can get your invoices paid on time just by using good customer service skills (no specialist skills needed).

Using customer service is a simple, gentle way to make sure you get paid on time and has the added benefit of keeping valuable customers for the long term. The best and least confronting way to get invoices paid is to engage your customer and build a positive working relationship with them throughout the sales process, so they value your service, like you, and *want* to pay you on time.

WHAT THIS BOOK *IS*

This book shows the busy small business owner the simple, practical customer service 'tweaks' they can make throughout their sales process to ensure they get paid by the due date. After making those 'tweaks' they won't have to worry about either poor cashflow or chasing unpaid invoices. They can focus on what they do best – selling more and growing their business.

Most small business owners will agree that sales are all about relationships: 'People buy from people they like'. Getting paid on time is also about relationships because 'people pay people they like' too. This book shows you the five steps to get customers to *want* to pay you on time, to give you repeat business, and to refer you to other businesses. This is exactly the process we followed in my business, with great success.

The five steps are:

1   How to set up your business for collections success.

2   How to feel 100% confident asking for payment.

3   The 'insider secret' and how to minimise problems that cause payment delays.

4   What to say, when, and to whom to get your invoices paid on time.

5   Red flags! How to spot one and what to do about it.

You'll learn all about these steps and how to implement them in this book. Just take the first of the five steps and watch the transformation. See your confidence grow daily. Feel relieved, cashed up, stress-free, and ready to focus on growth and profits, just the way I did.

> 'One of the biggest mistakes, but also the simplest to rectify, is not having simple processes and procedures in place that streamline your receivables communication with your clients.'
>
> *Sam Allert, Managing Director, Reckon*

You'll notice that throughout the book there are a few recurring themes, and I often refer to the same issue in a different context. That's because these are the most important aspects of getting paid, and they are relevant to many different parts of the process.

WHAT THIS BOOK *ISN'T*

This is *not* a book that involves strong-arm tactics, baseball bats or recovering bad debts. There are professional local and international businesses that specialise in the recovery of very overdue debts. Nor is this a 'dusty', hard-to-understand technical book that lists specific laws around collecting overdue payments.

THE MOST COMMON PAYMENT MYTHS AND MISTAKES

There are many myths surrounding the payment of invoices, particularly with small businesses – the biggest one is that customers simply don't *want* to pay, that they just want to hold on to their money. (See more about this in Step 3.) And there are many mistakes I've seen over and over again when businesses are trying to get paid.

> **Most of the worries small business owners have about getting invoices paid are actually myths or mistakes.**

Let's look at some of the most common payment myths and mistakes:

- 'If I ask the customer to pay they'll go to my competition.' **MYTH!**

- 'Asking for payment is always difficult – there's no easy way.' **MISTAKE!**

- 'If I ask the customer to pay they will get upset.' **MYTH!**

- 'Sending an email or statement is the best way to chase up overdue payments.' **MISTAKE!**

- 'Customers don't really want to pay.' **MYTH!**

- 'There's nothing I can do to make it any easier for my customers to pay on time.' **MISTAKE!**

- 'Asking customers to pay always makes me anxious. It's not possible to feel confident and prepared.' **MYTH!**

- 'If it becomes a bad debt, I've only lost the value of the invoice.' **BIG MISTAKE!**

- 'The longer I wait for payment, the more my customer will like me.' **MYTH!**

- 'Cashflow is a problem for all small businesses.' **MYTH!**

- 'There is no way that it can be fun asking customers to pay – it's agonising.' **MISTAKE!**

- 'You need collections training to know how to ask for payment.' **MISTAKE!**

- 'It's impossible to get hold of the right person.' **MISTAKE!**

- 'Asking for payment of an invoice can't ever be a win/win.' **MISTAKE!**

- 'Customers would never go out of their way to pay me.' **MISTAKE!**

- 'Talking to my customer face to face won't make any difference to how they pay me.' **MISTAKE!**

- 'It's the customer's fault they don't pay on time. There's nothing I can do about it.' **MYTH!**

- 'I don't have a valid reason to call my customer about my invoice before the due date.' **MISTAKE!**

This book is about dispelling these myths and mistakes, it explains why customers don't 'just pay', and shows the small business owner all the simple things they can put in place to reverse that.

WHY I WROTE THIS BOOK

I wrote this book for all those small business owners who have put their whole life and life savings into a business and risk seeing it fail because they don't know how to ask for payment of their invoices. If that describes you, I wrote this book especially for you.

Having spent 40 years – my whole career – working in and around getting invoices paid on time, I know why customers don't 'just pay', and I know all the simple things a small business owner can do to make sure customers do 'just pay'. I proved that in my own small business.

I spent the first half of my working life as a credit control and collections employee in multinational organisations in the UK, collecting invoice payments from corporates, utilities, SMEs and one-man bands. The second half of my career I spent starting, growing and then selling my own small business in Australia.

In my own business, I made many mistakes around getting paid and learnt from them (only after a cashflow near disaster!), eventually devising a simple five-step customer-service-based system to make sure our invoices got paid on time. From that day forward, my clients always paid on time.

Not having to worry about cashflow gave me the freedom to focus entirely on growth and profit, and I built one of the most profitable businesses in Australia. In this book I'm sharing my five-step system with you, so that you too can have great cashflow, more money in the bank and less money 'at risk'. Then you can focus your energies on what you are good at, the reason you started your business, and on growing your business and profits, rather than on chasing unpaid invoices or worrying about having enough cash in the bank to cover all your financial responsibilities.

My five-step system is based around my proven philosophy about being paid:

> The best, and least confronting, way to get invoices paid is to engage your customer and build a positive working relationship with them throughout the sales process. That way, customers get to value your service, like you and want to pay you on time.
>
> Using customer service is a simple, gentle way to make sure you get paid on time and has the added benefit of keeping valuable customers for the long term.

HOW TO SET UP YOUR BUSINESS FOR COLLECTIONS SUCCESS

'As with almost any problem, the best way to stop debt collection problems is before they start. The second-best solution is to identify a problem early.'

Dean Kaplan, President, The Kaplan Group

If you've ever chased an overdue invoice only to find the customer is 'sitting on it' because it's with the wrong person or it's got an error on it, you would know that's really infuriating. By the time you find out who to speak to, what the problem is, and sort it out, the invoice is seriously overdue, and you're irritated and exasperated and missing money from your bank account.

Late payment of invoices can cause serious cashflow issues for small business owners, sometimes so serious it can lead to potential business failure.

In my first year as a small business owner, I was so determined to make sales and learn how to run a business that I didn't have a clear focus on invoicing. The first time I focused on invoicing was when I realised that lots of our invoices weren't being paid and so I *had to* give them my complete and full attention!

A bit of research revealed that almost 50% of our invoices were being sent out with errors on them and according to research, that is the norm.

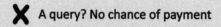

49% OF INVOICES HAVE ERRORS...

✘ A query? No chance of payment

At that stage in my business, I didn't own my home so I had no security to put up to get a loan. I had to make the business work with just the cash I initially put in and the income from the invoices, so I needed to solve this problem – and quickly!

Fortunately, all the errors we were making were small and I could see that by tweaking some areas of our admin, we could easily avoid making errors in future, so, I created an invoice checklist (see page 55) that we followed every time we created a new invoice in the future. That way, we made sure invoices were perfect before they were sent.

I changed the focus of the business from just *making a sale* to *making a sale that got paid*, and all we had to do was tweak a few simple administration tasks so that we set our customers up for payment success. By making sure their invoices were correct and with the right person in the right place, almost overnight we made it as easy as possible for our customers to pay on time.

Just those few steps improved our collection rates by over 50%. Big result. Interestingly, we also improved our customer relationships, which led to more orders, more profit and more referrals.

Having money continually flowing back into the business eased the pressure on me considerably, and I was able to focus all my energies on sales, profit and growing the business.

The following chapters show you the why and the how of setting your customers up for payment success. Step 1 involves just a little bit of planning, administration and focus.

1. BEGIN WITH THE END IN MIND

'As the director of a business, if you aren't
making a profit, you aren't doing your job.'

Michael Sheargold, CEO, trainer, coach and mentor to the
real estate sector (my first business coach)

Small business is hard. I know – I've had one.

Having a small business that's successful, makes a profit and becomes valuable enough for someone to want to buy, rather than just 'a job' for the owner, can be just a matter of learning how to 'tweak' a few areas – and getting paid on time is definitely one of those areas.

Let's face it, you've done your research and marketing to get the lead, worked hard to get the order, and you've done the job. You've issued the invoice … but have you been paid?

If you haven't been paid, you might as well have opened the window and thrown your cash out.

Most people don't start a business to lose money, but – although statistics vary – we know that the failure rate of businesses – because they run out of cash – is very high, leaving the owner worse off than before.

> **Why small businesses fail: insufficient capital, poor cashflow management***
>
> - 35% of businesses fail after two years
> - 50% of businesses fail after five years
> - 67% of businesses fail after ten years

People generally start a business to make money:

- to provide for themselves and their family
- to provide for themselves in retirement; and have the freedom to do what they want, when they want
- to sell the business and do something different
- to leave a legacy.

I started my business in my 40s after a divorce. I'd had a good job and my own home since I was in my 20s. Suddenly, at 40 I had no home, no job and very little money.

I realised then that I didn't have too many years to rebuild my life and provide for my future, so I started my business to provide myself with a big enough income so I could buy a home and feel secure again.

A couple of years after I started the business, I heard a successful business owner share how and why he had such a strong focus on profit. This is what he said:

> **'The only reason to have a business is to sell it.'**

(And he grew his profit and business further. So much so that, several years later, it became a public company.)

---

* National Federation of Independent Business.

I suddenly realised that companies buy *profitable* businesses, and that if I made good profits I'd be able to sell my business to fund my retirement. That, and being told that, as a business owner, I wasn't doing my job if I wasn't making a profit, was how and why I learned to focus on profit.

Getting invoices paid on time is one step towards making a healthy profit. If your invoices get paid on time you should have strong cashflow, so unless you want to invest a large sum in expansion or you are buying new equipment, you can run the business comfortably, paying staff, suppliers and yourself without having to make loan repayments and pay interest to the lender.

> 'It is not the employer who pays the wages. Employers only handle the money. It is the customer who pays the wages.'
>
> *Henry Ford, founder of The Ford Motor Company*

Business can be broken down to just two things, and for any business to thrive, there has to be a balance of the two:

1   providing services or goods

2   being paid for them.

All businesses exist to provide goods or a service and be paid for it, and it's hard to go wrong if you provide value to your customers (so long as you get paid of course!).

To provide for myself and make a profit so I could sell my business later, I had to find a way to do both.

Over time I learned that by giving customers exactly what they wanted (not more, or less, just exactly) and excellent service all through the sales process, we built strong relationships with them. They came to like us and value our service. As our relationship grew, we found they were much more likely to pay us before they paid other suppliers. You can think about it as providing a service to *enable* your customer to pay on time.

PEOPLE WE LIKE GET PAID FIRST

If people like you they pay you

And there were two added bonuses:

1   Our customers gave us more orders (instead of going to our competition), so we only had to spend minimal amounts on advertising and marketing to find new customers.

2   They referred us to other businesses (free marketing!).

Who would imagine that just some good old-fashioned customer service could have so many benefits? But it did, and my business survived, thrived, and made market-enviable profits for 15 years, until I sold it to an ASX-listed company.

In the next chapter we'll make a start by seeing if your trading terms are encouraging your customers to pay late.

KEY POINTS

- Providing goods or a service without being paid for it can lead to the loss of your business, possibly your home, or worse.

- Insufficient capital and poor cashflow are among the biggest reasons for business failure.

- Providing outstanding service to customers can easily improve profits by encouraging them to pay on time (providing good service is so much cheaper and less risky than having heaps of unpaid invoices and having to take out a loan to pay your staff, suppliers and yourself).

- Because of your great service, customers get to like you and like working with you and that encourages them to reorder and recommend you to their business friends (so much easier and cheaper than looking for new business).

TO DO

1 Take 10 minutes now to make a list of the 10 easiest ways you can provide a better service to your customers.

2 Implement your new improved customer service strategies and watch all the positive outcomes.

2. ARE YOUR TERMS OF TRADE ENCOURAGING CUSTOMERS TO PAY LATE?

TRADING TERMS or TERMS OF TRADE

Do your customers owe you lots of money? *Too much* money?

Your payment terms could be at fault.

If it's a constant struggle in your business to have enough cash to pay your staff, your suppliers and yourself, you may need to rethink your payment terms.

A small business owner friend of mine, Stuart, told me recently that his terms were '30 days net' but he was waiting up to 60 days to get his invoices paid. Generally, 30 days net is interpreted as 'the end of the month following the date of the invoice'. So, for example:

'30 days net' invoice: 1 July to 31 August = 62 days

When I asked why he'd chosen terms of 30 days net, he said he didn't really know what terms to choose so he'd picked 30 days net out of thin air! After I explained that this gave customers an opportunity to take 60 days or more to pay, he changed his terms to 7 days from date of invoice.

Not long afterwards he told me that his very next customer had paid 'upfront', before he had even provided his service!

WHAT DOES 'TERMS OF TRADE' REALLY MEAN?

Simplified, terms of trade are saying:

'When you order from us, we will supply you. And after receiving those goods or the service, you will pay us in X days.'

WHAT ARE THE RIGHT TERMS FOR YOU?

Two things are important when deciding on what trading terms to offer your customers:

- **What terms are your competitors offering?** If you offer a better service, perhaps you can ask for better terms. That's exactly what I did. Sometimes all you need to do is ask.

- **What are the best terms you can offer customers and still have a totally sustainable business?** A business that has enough cashflow to be comfortable enough to pay your staff and suppliers – and yourself?

ARE YOUR TERMS
THE RIGHT TERMS FOR YOU?

The longer your terms

=

The more of your $ outstanding

=

The more of your $ at risk!

The longer your terms of trade – that is, the greater the number of days – the more money you will have outstanding and at risk, and the more money you will have to put in, or leave in, your business bank account to be able to pay your bills, your staff and yourself.

In my business, we had two different areas of business so two different types of invoices with different terms of trade for each:

1 **Weekly invoices with terms of 7 days from date of invoice.** Invoices we sent out on a Friday, we expected to be paid by the following Friday.

2 **30 days from date of invoice.** We sent those invoices out immediately the work was completed and expected them to be paid 30 days later; invoice billed on 15 May, payment due on 15 June.

Most customers bought both services from us and so received the two different types of invoices. To make life easier for our customers and to average things out, we gave ourselves a target of collecting payment of all our invoices in an average of 24 days from the invoice date. Because we needed to have money continually flowing back into the business to cover our huge weekly outgoings, we tracked our success every day.

Our part-time administrator followed our simple collections policy and five-step process, and got all our invoices paid on average between 22 and 25 days. That was considered outstanding. It was the very best in our industry.

EXAMPLES OF COMMON PAYMENT TERMS

Here are some examples of common payment terms:

- Payment in advance ('upfront').

- 50% payment in advance – 50% due on delivery.

- Payment due on delivery (cash, credit card or bank transfer).

- 7 days from invoice date (billed Monday, due the following Monday).

- 14 days from invoice date (billed Monday, due Monday 14 days later).

- 30 days from invoice date (invoice dated 5 March, due for payment by 5 April).

- 30 days net (due at the end of the month following the invoice date; invoice dated 1 March, payment due on 30 April).

- 45 days net (due 45 days after the end of the billing month; billed 6 June, payment due 45 days after 30 June).

- 60 days net (due at the end of the second month following the invoice date; invoice dated 1 March due for payment 31 May).

Choosing the right trading terms is critical for any business. Use the table at the end of this chapter to analyse your own trading terms, to decide if you should make some changes.

In the next chapter, we'll look at how, when everyone in the business focuses on great customer service, it's so much easier to get paid on time.

KEY POINTS

- Your trading terms can make a huge difference to your cashflow.

- Getting your invoices paid earlier could just be a matter of tweaking your trading terms and making the payment date really clear on your invoice (see chapter 9, 'How to create an invoice that gets paid on time: a "killer" invoice').

TO DO

1   If you'd like to get your invoices paid earlier, review your trading terms and decide if they are right for you. If they are not, you can make some changes (just the way Stuart did).

2   Use a table like the one following to work out what terms you could have to get customers to pay earlier, so that you have less money outstanding (and at risk).

3   Make your terms of trade and the payment due date clear and prominent on your invoice.

ANALYSING YOUR TERMS OF TRADE

1. What trading terms do our competitors offer customers?	
2. Do we really need to match our competitors' terms? (Maybe we offer a better service than our competitors?)	
3. Which customers could we (and should we) ask to pay before the delivery or service (upfront)?	
4. Which customers do pay on time? (Why is that?)	
5. Which customers don't pay on time? (Why is that?)	
6. Can we change our terms now for new customers?	
7. Which customers pay us so late that we don't make a profit on transactions with them?	
8. Is it worthwhile offering a discount for early payment? Would we still make a profit?	
9. What payment terms shall we adopt?	
10. How do we warn customers that we will change our terms? • Three months' notice? • The beginning of the financial year? • The beginning of the next quarter?	

Download this table here: https://janreeves.com/bookbonuses-dl/

3. HAVING THE RIGHT FOCUS: THE CUSTOMER

'Revolve your world around the customer
and more customers will revolve around you.'

Heather Williams, Customer Service Leader, British Airways

Business is basically one company ('the supplier') providing goods or services to a second company or person ('the customer') and the supplier being paid for it. Within that basic framework, here's what the two parties want:

What a customer wants from their supplier:

- Exactly what they ordered.

- To feel valued and welcome.

What a supplier wants from their customer:

- To pay their bill on time.

- To reorder.

- To recommend them to other businesses.

Business owners work hard to get a new customer on board, often winning them away from the competition. To make sure the business gets value and profit out of every transaction, *everyone employed in any organisation* must be there to be of service to the customer and to make the customer feel valued.

TOP SERVICE = CUSTOMERS LIKE YOU

Great Customer Service

If there are only two key aspects of business – providing exactly what the customer wants and getting paid for it – then everyone needs to focus on two things:

1 Providing exactly the goods or services that the customer ordered.

2 Providing the service, throughout the whole sales to order process and beyond, that enables your customer to pay on time (and hopefully reorder).

Having existing customers that reorder is a very cost-effective way to grow a business. The time and costs involved in finding a new customer is widely accepted to be six to seven times the cost of supplying an existing customer. Imagine then how much more profitable repeat business is.

After making a sale, we want our money and another order. So, after setting our customer up for success, the next step is servicing them, so they never want to leave us and buy from our competitors.

KEY POINTS

- Out of 10, how important is a sale to you?

- Out of 10, how important is a sale to you that never gets paid?

TO DO

Decide what the focus of your business really is. Is it to make money? How will you do that? What's important to you:

1 Making sales?

2 Getting paid for the sales you make and making profits?

4. HAVING THE RIGHT ATTITUDE: SERVICE WITH A SMILE

'If it's going to be, it's up to me.'

Robert H. Schuller, motivational speaker, author and pastor

GIVE YOUR CUSTOMER YOUR COMPLETE ATTENTION

Talking to Customers = Strong Business Relationships

You may not have thought of it this way before, but as the business owner, the person who is most interested and has the most to gain by getting your invoices paid on time is you. No-one is more interested than you are. There's a 99% chance that the only person who will go *out of their way* to make sure your invoice gets paid and gets paid on time is you.

How often has a customer called you to say, 'We'd like to pay your invoice on time, but we don't have it. We've asked everyone in our company, but no-one seems to know where it is. Perhaps you've sent it to the wrong company or wrong address'? It just doesn't happen.

Can you see the way this is going? There's no getting away from it: making sure your invoices get paid is totally your responsibility.

If your invoice has a mistake on it, there's about a 10% chance your customer will call and let you know. The other 90% of the time your customer will wait for you to call to ask why it hasn't been paid yet before they tell you there's a problem with your invoice. They are spending their time working to make their company successful and profitable, not helping suppliers.

Since you are the person most interested in getting your invoice paid, you have to find a way to make sure your customer puts your invoices to the top of their payment pile. That doesn't mean getting on the phone and blasting them – that's how you can lose a valuable customer,.

So, how do you do this?

HOW TO MAKE YOUR CLIENTS FEEL LOVED – AND WHY YOU SHOULD

No-one likes dealing with grumpy people. You certainly wouldn't pay grumpy people first. Not many people would. We all like to pay people we like first.

None of us want to call people who are grumpy either. I've seen admin people grumpily treat valuable customers like 'the enemy' because they have an invoice outstanding. That's a good way to put a customer 'off side'.

We all want to avoid interacting with miserable people, which means if there's a problem with your invoice and you are generally grumpy, miserable or unhelpful, your customer is not going to call you about it.

The way to ensure your customers want to call you (and pay you) is to make sure they always feel welcome when they contact your business. So, how do you make sure your customers are always happy to pick up the phone to speak to you? It's really not that hard, there's no costs involved, and everyone gains. Here's some ideas for you and your team:

- Always give your customer your full attention. Don't be checking your email, drinking coffee or chewing anything while you're talking to them. They will be able to tell you are distracted.

- Always use your customer's name. If you don't know it, simply ask at the beginning of the call.

- Positive language makes communications flow. Adopt a 'can-do' attitude and use expressions like 'how can I help you?'.

- Say 'yes' as often as you can, and you'll stand out from the crowd.

- Negative language hinders communications, so keep 'no', 'not', and 'never' out of your conversation.

- If a customer asks how you are, regardless of how you feel, tell them you are 'good' or 'very well', or 'excellent' even.

- Return customer calls promptly and with grace.

- Listen carefully to what your customer is saying and don't interrupt or pre-empt.

- If a client calls at an inconvenient time, explain that you have some other commitments right now and make a time for you to call them back. (And make sure you do!)

- End your call by wishing your customer a 'great afternoon' or a 'nice evening', and you can even say 'looking forward to speaking with you/catching up with you again tomorrow' or 'next week/month'.

Having everybody in your business committed to providing 'service with a smile' is another tweak you can make that will see you get paid. It takes no more time, costs nothing, and has lots of benefits for the giver and receiver: everyone has a nicer day.

When your customers enjoy interacting with your business they'll be much more likely to pay you on time or let you know if there's a problem.

KEY POINTS

- Why do some business owners work hard to get a sale, and then as soon as the goods or services have been supplied stop all communication and treat the customer like 'the enemy'? This is a great way to lose clients.

- Making clients feel valued and appreciated by giving them great service will pay you back dividends. They'll be more likely to pay you on time and reorder, and you'll feel great too.

TO DO

If this is a whole new concept for you, to remind yourself what to do to build relationships with customers so they feel welcome and valuable, put a couple of large signs up to remind you and your team (I do this when I'm trying to adopt a new habit). You could write something like this:

'What do I need to do today to build stronger business relationships with my customers?'

Or:

'What is it that I need to do today to start to get my customers to like me?'

5. HOW TO KEEP YOUR COOL AND WHY IT'S SO IMPORTANT

'Give people the benefit of the doubt, dear.'

E.J.W. Reeves
(my Mum – and we all know Mums are always right)

How often do you get mad because a customer hasn't paid on time or furious when several customers haven't paid? You feel frustrated and cross because you've worked hard to keep your end of the bargain. You've fulfilled the customer's order. Maybe you even went out of your way to fulfil an urgent or difficult order.

It's easy to think the worst – that they are holding on to their money on purpose. It's maddening! You have bills to pay. You've got rent and wages and you need to pay yourself too – anyone would feel mad.

'Almost 50% of small business owners have sacrificed their own salary for the good of the business in recent months.'

USA Today *Small Business Barometer*

Well, this is a good time to take a deep breath, keep your cool and consider a few facts:

- No-one can ever *force* a customer to pay. It's just not physically possible (not without running the risk of imprisonment). You must find a better way.

- You don't want to upset and lose your customer, having worked hard and spent money getting them on board.

- You really want this customer to keep buying from you – not from your competitor.

- There can be many *legitimate reasons* why your customer hasn't paid.

If you get on the phone and lose your cool you will be doing yourself a great disservice. You get mad at your customer; your customer gets mad at you. That doesn't get you anywhere.

Instead, think of it as an opportunity.

This could be a great opportunity to make your relationship with the customer stronger. If you make the relationship stronger you could get them to pay on time in the future and get more business from them. This is exactly what I did in my small business. This is one of the ways I completely self-funded my business and made it much more profitable at the same time.

When one of our customers hadn't paid, instead of losing our cool, we made a phone call using our best customer service attitude – service with a smile. We gave the customer the benefit of the doubt until we really knew what is was at the customer's end that was preventing payment.

> **Always keep your cool when dealing with customers.**

This was around the time we figured out that over half our invoices had an error on them. And even worse, sometimes when we called to ask a customer why they hadn't paid their invoice, we found out that the customer had already called us and left a message to report they had a query, but the message hadn't been passed on to the right person. (Has that happened to you? Me too.)

One time when our computer system failed, the last few phone message notes sent out from our receptionist that day were lost. One was a note to me saying that one of our relatively new customers would like to speak to me about an invoice. Of course, I hadn't called back because I hadn't received the note, and a few days later our administrator called them to ask why they hadn't paid their invoice.

Fortunately, she framed the call as an enquiry, but just imagine if we had called our new customer and blasted them for not paying, only to find out they were waiting for us to get back to them. It would have damaged the relationship almost before it had started, and then we would have been back to the expensive process of trying to find a replacement customer.

Instead of ringing up with a confrontational attitude, we said something like this:

'I know we shipped those goods on [date]. We thought you must have received them, so we issued our invoice #12678 on [date]. We don't appear to have received payment yet, and we don't know of any problem or query. Is there something wrong?'

Until you are certain that your customer is deliberately withholding payment, stay calm and polite while you're trying to find out what the payment hold-up is. Give your customer 'the benefit of the doubt'. Once you know what it is holding up your payment, you can find the right way to handle it so your customer *can* pay.

KEY POINTS

- Always give customers the benefit of the doubt.

- Until you are sure that your customer is withholding payment just to hold on to their cash, treat non-payment of an invoice as an enquiry.

- Find out what is causing the hold-up. At least 50% of the time there will be a reason that you can easily solve.

TO DO

Pick five customers with an overdue invoice and make 'exploratory' customer service calls. Adapt the example earlier in this chapter to suit you. Start to analyse what the underlying reason is for the late payments.

6. HOW TO TRAIN NEW CUSTOMERS TO PAY ON TIME

'Customer service should not be a department.
It should be the entire company.'

*Tony Hsieh, CEO of Zappos, online shoe and clothing
retail giant (subsidiary of Amazon)*

Training new customers to pay on time is a great way to start to make a few changes to your admin processes as you work your way towards getting *all* customers to pay on time. A little 'upfront' work can make a huge difference to whether you get paid on time, or your invoices end up at the bottom of the payment pile.

Start training your new customer by making a cheerful customer service call to introduce yourself before you send out their first invoice. Once you've established a little bit of a rapport you can find out what you need to know to streamline your delivery, invoicing and payment process. This is great customer service, and your customer will think you are really efficient. It will also help you to avoid making a mistake on your invoice which could hold up your payment later on.

I used this strategy to charm my new customers and get the relationship off to a positive, flying start. Once you've established a pleasant working relationship, it's so much easier to contact customers to talk through any challenges that might occur later on while you are fulfilling their order.

PUT YOUR CUSTOMER AT EASE

✓ Break the ice
✓ Be friendly and engaging
✓ Positive and professional
✓ Genuinely complimentary
✓ Say thanks

MAKING INTRODUCTORY CALLS TO NEW CLIENTS

Here's a few examples of introductory calls that have worked well for me.

Before you send a new customer their first invoice:

'Hello Charles, my name is Jan Reeves and I'll be looking after your account. I've set up the account and I have your first invoice here.

Before I send the invoice through to you, I thought I'd check that we have all the right contact details and we've included all the information that you need in the invoice. Are you the right person to talk to regarding that?'

If the invoice has already been sent:

'Alex, Hello. It's Jan Reeves here from Get Paid!

Your company recently purchased some "Super Widgets" from us and we've sent our invoice SW19000 to cover that.

I'll be looking after your account, so I thought I'd call to introduce myself to you and make sure you have the invoice and everything you need from us.

Then you can ask:

1   *'Do you have that invoice? SW19000?' (Pause for them to say yes or no.)*

2   *'Does it have all the information you need?' (The use of 'you' is good here – I'm helping* **you***. Pause for them to say yes or no.)*

3   *'Has it been signed off yet/authorised for payment yet?' (Pause for them to say yes or no.)*

A cheerful introductory phone call with a new client is non-confrontational and can be the start of a positive relationship. When you have already established a positive relationship with your customer, it will be much easier to sort out any problems that might arise in the future.

KEY POINTS

- Get to know your contact in your customer's business at a positive time. Before you send your first invoice is a good time, then you can make sure you include everything the customer needs to see on your invoice.

- If you establish a good relationship at a positive time, it'll be much easier to chat to the person you already know if something challenging comes up during the sales or getting paid process.

TO DO

Decide when the best time is to make first contact with your new customer; for example, just before you send out their first invoice. (See the checklist on page 51.)

Download this checklist here:
https://janreeves.com/bookbonuses-dl/

7. HOW INVOICE AND ACCOUNTING SOFTWARE CAN HELP YOU GET PAID

Some small businesses still prepare invoices in MS Word and keep track of invoices and payments with an Excel spreadsheet. This can work well if you have just a few transactions, but if you have more, there is invoicing software available that will help you create invoices and reminders more quickly, more easily and more efficiently.

Some of the most popular are FreshBooks, Wave, Xero, MYOB, Zoho and QuickBooks (Intuit), who all offer phone or chat support (or both). Mostly, there's a small monthly charge, but one or two are free.

To find software to suit your business and pocket, you can check out summaries of what each of them do and reviews of them online. Things to take note of are what size your company is, and if you sell products – so maybe need to track inventory – or services – where you might need to track hours.

Some time-saving tasks accounting software can do are:

- create estimates and quotes

- create invoices from quotes

- accept payments online

- send out reminders and statements

- create recurring transactions

- create reports (accounts receivable, accounts payable, cash at bank, profit and loss, and much more).

Accounting software can also record and track all your transactions with your customers – both for your customer and for you, the business owner – and that makes it much easier to keep track of which customers haven't paid so you can decide what to do about it. So long as the operator sends out correct invoices, invoicing software can encourage customers to pay by providing them with lots of easy payment options.

A word of warning here. Although accounting software can make accounting tasks easier, it *can't* make people pay, make them pay on time, or make them want to pay. If you want customers to *want* to pay you on time, reorder, and become a 'raving fan' so they start to do your marketing for you by referring you to other businesses, you need to unleash your inner superhero customer service self and engage with them.

KEY POINTS

- Accounting software can help you create invoices and reminders more quickly, more easily and more efficiently.

- It can also create dynamic reports at the press of a button, so you can keep a daily, weekly and monthly track of what each customer owes you and how old the amount is.

- Warning: although accounting software can make some tasks much quicker and easier, it can't *make people pay, make them want to pay or make them pay on time.*

TO DO

1 If you don't already use accounting software, look at reviews of the most popular ones on the internet and decide which one would best suit your business and pocket.

2 If you are already using accounting software:

- Make sure you have a strategy in place to integrate creating 'killer invoices' (chapter 9) so your customer starts to get to know you in a non-confrontational environment (before you send out their first invoice) and you know your perfectly correct invoices are reaching the right person.

- Make your 'courtesy calls' (see chapter 18) to enhance your customer service superhero status and make sure there's nothing to stop your invoice being paid on time.

8. A SAMPLE COLLECTIONS POLICY, AND WHY YOU NEED ONE

'Late payments? Many SME owners neglect to set up a
clear invoice management strategy from the get-go.'

A.J. Singh, Managing Director, EzyCollect

Alongside trading terms that are competitive, so they'll help your business survive and thrive, you need to have a collections policy as well.

There's no point in working hard to implement a sales and marketing strategy so you can sell your goods and services to customers if you don't have a strategy to make sure you get each invoice paid too. A sale that isn't paid for is worthless and will cost you much more than the value of the invoice. Too many unpaid invoices will be fatal to your business.

> A sale is only a sale when your invoice has been
> paid and your money is in your bank account.

Your collections policy simply states **what you will action and when** to make sure you get your invoices paid.

Your policy can be brief but should have an objective and detail both the strategies and the timing you'll use to make sure your invoices are paid when you want them paid.

Here's an example of the one that I used in my business.

Collections policy objective: *That all invoices are paid within a maximum of 21 days from the invoice date.*

All verbal interactions and agreements with the customer regarding our invoices must be recorded, in detail, in their file for future reference. Notes must be accessible to everyone in the company in case they need access when speaking to the customer (for example, invoice numbers, queries and promised payment dates).

1. Enter payments into accounting system.
2. Mark off today's paid invoices.
3. Make 'courtesy' calls on current invoices.
4. Make collection calls on invoices 1–7 days overdue.
5. Make follow-up calls on invoices 8–14 days overdue.
6. Invoices 22+ days overdue: don't delay – consider alternative action; visit, stop supply, pass to collection agency.

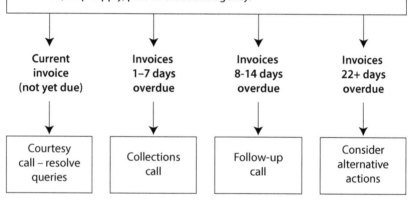

Current invoice (not yet due)	Invoices 1–7 days overdue	Invoices 8-14 days overdue	Invoices 22+ days overdue
Courtesy call – resolve queries	Collections call	Follow-up call	Consider alternative actions

* * *

Learning to think about a sale as a whole transaction – that it is really *only a valuable sale when it's paid* – is fundamental to the success of your business.

The next stage is to give your invoice the best chance of being paid by making sure it is 100% correct, and we cover that in chapter 9, 'How to create an invoice that gets paid on time: a "killer" invoice'.

KEY POINTS

- Not having a plan, a strategy and a system to get your invoices paid can result in disaster.

- The biggest disaster is loss of your business and potential bankruptcy, which might cause the loss of your home too.

TO DO

1   Decision time: How long you are prepared to wait for payment of your invoices?

2   Create a simple strategy, like the one in this chapter, to make getting paid as important as making a sale. After all, one without the other is a potential disaster.

9. HOW TO CREATE AN INVOICE THAT GETS PAID ON TIME: A 'KILLER' INVOICE

'If you don't have time to do it right,
when will you have time to do it over?'

John Wooden, Hall of Fame basketball player/coach

How many times have you called to chase payment of an overdue invoice and heard your customer say:

'Oh, we don't have that invoice.'

Or:

'No, we haven't paid that because the calculation's wrong'?

Or, you find out long after the invoice should have been paid that it's been sent to the wrong person, the wrong address, or the order or reference number is missing.

According to a 2015 survey by receivables management software company TermSync, a massive 49% of invoices aren't paid on time because there's an error somewhere.

INVOICES WITH ERRORS DON'T GET PAID!

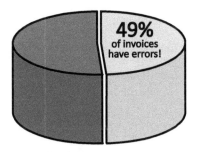

49%
of invoices
have errors!

The error might be tiny and anywhere on the invoice, but any error gives your customer a perfectly legitimate reason to hold on to their money. *Your* money.

In my small business, our customers paid by the due date, but only because I had learnt the hard way that invoices with queries on them don't get paid.

We often had quite complicated calculations on our invoices, and one small error meant that payment would be delayed. One day we sent 10 invoices to the same customer and they all had the same incorrect calculation. We didn't find out until after the invoices should have been paid which delayed the payment of about $10,000 for over two weeks. That cost us in two ways:

- it made us look inefficient

- we were short of $10,000 in our bank account.

It was a double loss for my business.

After that, we always made it a priority to ensure our invoices were 100% correct. That they were 'killer' invoices. From that point, customers had hardly any queries on invoices that might delay their payment.

When an invoice is perfect – a 'killer' invoice – it's got the best chance of being paid on time. Killer invoices:

- have *all* the details the customer needs

- show clear, *unmissable* trading terms

- show the payment *due date clearly*

- are *sent out immediately* after the work is completed or the goods are sent

- are *clear* and easy to read so it's easy to find information

- have the correct pricing and calculations

- are addressed to exactly the right person at the right location.

When you send out 100% correct invoices, you're removing the opportunity for your customer to have a reason not to pay on time.

'KILLER' INVOICES GET PAID SOONER

KILLER INVOICES

Make 'Excuses Not to Pay' VANISH

Once you make a point of sending out only 100% correct 'killer' invoices you'll save yourself heaps of time and frustration, and have a much better chance of being paid on time.

There are so many benefits of 'killer' invoices:

- You won't have to chase up so many customers for payment – very frustrating!

- You won't have to stop what you're doing to resolve queries on invoices.

- You'll have more time to grow your business.

- As more customers pay on time you'll have more money in the bank.

- It will improve relationships with your customers as they will be impressed by your customer service and efficiency.

Those are pretty compelling reasons to spend a little bit more time just making sure your invoices are 100% correct before you send them out.

KEY POINTS

- Invoices that have even tiny errors will almost certainly never be paid.

- If your invoices have errors, most likely your customers won't call you to let you know.

- You will only get to know about invoice errors when you call to ask why you haven't been paid and then you'll have to spend time correcting the error. You'll be frustrated because you haven't been paid and your customer won't be best pleased because you've caused them additional admin time. That's a negative environment in which to interact with your customer.

TO DO

Decide on and list the five key admin processes you need to change to make sure you send out only 100% correct invoices.

10. STEPS TO TAKE *BEFORE* YOU WRITE YOUR 'KILLER' INVOICE

KILLER INVOICE = PERFECT INVOICE

The idea is to send out *perfect* invoices. Invoices that don't get held up for payment because of a query. Invoices that make excuses not to pay vanish.

* Clear, easy to read

* All the right information needed for approval

* Correct pricing and calculations

* Exactly the right person at the right location.

INVOICES FOR NEW CUSTOMERS

With new customers, make a customer service call before you send out the first invoice. Introduce yourself and gather all the information you need, and your customer needs, to make sure you send them a perfect invoice, and the invoice goes to the person who has the authority to either pay it or authorise it for payment.

By confirming with your customer *exactly* who the invoice should be addressed to and the *exact* address it should go to, and by asking 'what else do they need to see on it', you'll be presenting yourself and your company as very service-oriented and creating perfect invoices.

You can use this call as an opportunity to start building your relationship with the customer. You could say something like this:

'Hello Angela, my name is Jan Reeves from Get Paid!

Your company has recently made a purchase from us and I understand you look after all invoices and payments – is that right?

I'm just setting up your account now and want to make sure that your invoices go straight to the right person and have all the information on them that you need. Have you got two minutes to run through that with me now?'

If they don't have time now, you can ask:

'When *would be a good time?'*

Asking someone 'when' is an 'open' question. Asking an 'open' question is a powerful way to get someone to give you an answer. Just pause (leave it 'open') after you ask the question and your customer will fill in the gap by telling you a good time.

The pause can feel a little uncomfortable, but just stay with it, because it's also uncomfortable for your customer, and because it's a little uncomfortable they'll fill the pause 'gap' with the information you've asked for and you stay in control of the conversation.

Open questions are great to use in all sorts of situations when you're trying to find answers or information. (See more about asking powerful 'open' questions in chapter 22.)

When the time is right for your client, you can run through your checklist with them. You can use this one as a guide and add in any particular points that you need to clarify.

Invoice creation checklist:

1 Goods or services delivery address

2 Invoicing address

3 Address invoice to the attention of ....

4 Order number

5 Special instructions

6 Invoice number

7 Invoice date

8 Date of delivery of service

9 Quantities

10 Item codes (if any)

11 Description of goods or service

12 Unit price

13 Total and sub-totals

14 Tax

15 Grand total

16 Terms of trade

17 Payment due date

18 Invoice contact details

19 Payment options

Download this checklist here: https://janreeves.com/bookbonuses-dl/

See more examples of what to say to train new customers to pay on time in chapter 6.

INVOICES FOR CUSTOMERS THAT CONTINUALLY PAY LATE

Calling your late-paying customers before you send out a new invoice to them is a wonderful opportunity to find out why they always pay late. Use the call as an opportunity to improve or build your relationship with the customer.

You could say something like this:

'Hello James. My name's Jan Reeves from Get Paid! I usually look after your account.

'I've got an invoice here that I'm just about to send out to you. There are also one or two old items on your account that I'm not sure about and would like to run through with you. I'm just wondering if our invoices are going to the right person in your company. Have you got two minutes to run through that with me now?'

And then run through your checklist.

If they don't have time now, you can ask:

'When *would be a good time?'*

LARGE-VALUE INVOICES: THE CRUCIAL STEPS TO TAKE

Large-value invoices are too important to be left to chance and must definitely be 100% correct and sent to the right person. Only send large-value invoices when you have gone through the checklist and you're sure the invoice is perfect before it leaves you.

What is a 'large value' invoice?

A large-value invoice in your business might be totally different to another business. As an example, in my business, during a month we sent out about 400 invoices, each with a value of between $700 to $1000. In the same month we also sent out 20 or 30 'large-value' invoices with a value of between $5,000 and $20,000.

Making a mistake on a 'smaller value' invoice would only hold up payment of $700 to $1000. If we made a mistake on a 'large-value' invoice, it held up payment of between $5,000 and $20,000. That would have made a much bigger dent in our bank balance.

In the next chapter I show you step by step how to create your 'killer' invoices.

KEY POINT

Use a checklist to make sure all your invoices are error-free. Invoices without errors get paid faster.

TO DO

1   With new customers, make a service call before sending out their first invoice and go through the invoice checklist with them.

2   Make a list of the top five customers that always pay late (especially if they always raise queries on invoices). Make a service call to them and go through the checklist to make sure you get their invoices correct in future. If they continue to pay late, you can consider stopping supplies or visiting them if they are a valuable customer (see chapter 40).

3   Decide what constitutes a 'large-value' invoice in your business: is it $1000, $5000, $10,000? Make a fail-safe plan so they are double-checked for errors before sending to clients.

---

11. WHAT TO INCLUDE ON ALL YOUR INVOICES TO GET PAID PROMPTLY

'If you don't get it right, what's the point?'

Michael Cimino, film director, screenwriter, producer and author

After making your customer service call and working your way through the checklist in the previous chapter, you are ready to write your 'killer' invoice.

In this chapter we'll look at the type of template we set up in our accounting software. You might need to tweak it a little bit to suit your particular business.

If you create a 'killer' template (you can download a Word template later in this chapter or use the template in your accounting software), and use it to create all your invoices, you can be quite sure in future that your invoice has gone to the right person, at the right address, that the calculations are correct, and it has every piece of information on it that your customer needs. That way, it's unlikely to be held up for payment because of an error.

Most invoicing software – such as Xero or MYOB – will allow you to create invoice templates, so if you are using one of those programs, you should really only have to go through the invoice set up process once (or a few times if you have different types of invoices).

Once your templates are set up correctly, it should be very easy for you to create and send out 'killer' invoices.

Let's have a look at what you need on your killer invoices. I've broken the invoice down into three parts.

Part 1 focuses on three very important things – making sure:

- your invoice contains **exactly the right address** – so many don't, and it wastes time

- your invoice gets to **exactly the right person** – the person who can pay it or authorise it to be paid

- your customer is quite clear that **they owe you money**, either for goods you have shipped or a service you have provided.

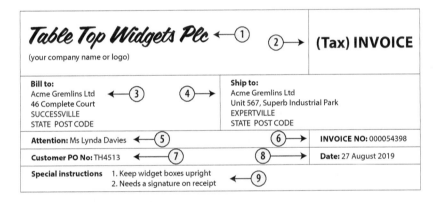

1   Your company name or your logo.

2   Write INVOICE in large bold letters (in Australia, if you are registered for GST you must write 'TAX INVOICE').

3   Fill in the 'Bill to' address (generally where your customer's accounts department is).

4   Fill in the 'Ship to' address (where the delivery was made).

5   If you have a contact name, insert it here.

6   Enter your invoice number.

7   If you have a purchase order number from your customer, enter it here. If not, enter the date the order was placed with you.

8   Enter today's date. (You should send out invoices immediately after the goods are sent or your service is delivered – the same day, if possible.)

9   Enter any special instructions your customer gave you or any important note(s) relating to the order or invoice.

Part 2 focuses on the next three important things: what you've provided and what your customer owes you. It includes:

• exactly **what you delivered** and how much you are charging your customer

• the **taxes you are required to collect** on behalf of the government

• the total **your customer owes you**.

Quantity	Item code	Description	Unit price	Total
100	AF63	Widgets – green laminate	0.93	93.00
300	AF97	Widgets – brass	0.99	297.00
1	CD794	Machine to turn widgets	657.00	657.00
1	TR03	3-hour training course on site on 19 August 2018 Participants: Grace Shearer and Michael Mitchell	350.00	350.00
1	SVE004	Service call out 24 August 2019	120.00	120.00

⑩ ⑪ ⑫ ⑬ ⑭

Thank you for choosing *Table Top Widgets Plc* ← ⑮

⑯ →	Sub total	$1,517.00
⑰ →	GST @ 10%	$151.70
⑱ →	Total	$1,668.70

10 Enter the quantity you provided.

11 If you have an item code or reference, enter it here.

12 Describe the goods or service.

13 Enter the unit price (how much the items are each).

14 Multiply the number shipped by the unit price.

15 Write a message of thanks to your customer.

16 Place the subtotal here.

17 Calculate the taxes you are required to collect on behalf of the government. (In Australia invoices are legally required to show the amount of GST included in the invoice.)

18 Enter the total your customer owes you.

Part 3 focuses on the four things you need to display to get paid quickly. It includes:

- your **trading terms**

- the **date your customer needs to pay** your invoice by

- the **name of a contact** in your organisation in the event of a query

- payment methods and details so your customer's **payment can reach you as quickly as possible**.

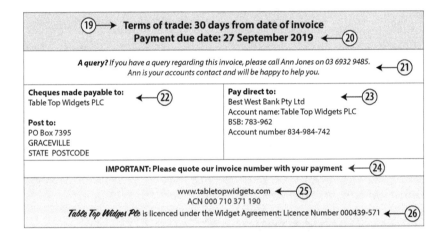

19 Enter your trading terms for this shipment or service. (Use '**From Date of Invoice**' rather than '**Net**'.)

20 Write the **exact payment due date** clearly so it can't be overlooked or mistaken.

21 Make it easy for your customer to know who to contact if they do have a query (but they shouldn't if the invoice is 100% correct!).

22 Make it clear who cheques should be made out to and where they should be posted to.

23 Encourage customers to pay directly into your bank account (saves you time and money). List here all your bank details, and any other payment options you offer.

24 Ask your customer to include your invoice number with their payment.

25 Include your web address.

26 Display your business legal credentials. (In Australia, your invoices must include your ABN if you have one.)

WHERE TO PLACE YOUR PAYMENT TERMS TO GET PAID FAST

I learnt this tip from receiving invoices from suppliers when I first started my business: if it wasn't really clear and obvious when I should pay the invoice, it went to the bottom of the pile.

That taught me a lesson.

I decided to create my invoices so that trading terms and the due date were really easy to see.

Trading terms and the payment date on 'killer' invoices are impossible to miss – see the previous image at numbers 19 and 20.

KILLER INVOICE TEMPLATE

This invoice template has been designed so that all the pieces of information your customer needs are easy for them to find. When you send your perfect invoice to exactly the right person at the right address, you're already streets ahead of your competition.

Download this template here: https://janreeves.com/bookbonuses-dl/

* * *

Can you see where this is heading?

So far, we have looked at some easy admin processes you can 'tweak' to put yourself in a more powerful position to get paid on time.

You are starting to build a relationship with your customer in a positive environment and then you're minimising the chances of an invoice getting 'stuck' on someone's desk because they don't know what to do with it or it has an error on it.

Errors on invoices are always your responsibility even if it's your customer's fault, because if something isn't right, your customer has a legitimate excuse to hold on to their money.

In later chapters, we dive further into looking after your customers so they get to like you even more. You will see how taking a couple of small 'customer service' steps can minimise any problems that might delay your payment.

KEY POINTS

- Errors on invoices are always your responsibility even if it's your customer's fault, because if something on your invoice isn't right, your customer has a legitimate excuse to hold on to their money.

- If your invoices have errors, most likely your customers won't call you to let you know. You will only get to know when you haven't been paid and then you'll be spending time making good the errors so your customer *can* pay.

- Trading terms and the due date of the invoice should be easy for your customer to see at a glance, otherwise your invoice could go on the bottom of the payment pile.

TO DO

1 Look at the example invoice in this chapter or download a copy of my invoice template here: https://janreeves. com/bookbonuses-dl/

2 If you are using accounting software, add in any key components that you might need.

Table Top Widgets Plc
(your company name or logo)

(Tax) INVOICE

Bill to:
Acme Gremlins Ltd
46 Complete Court
SUCCESSVILLE
STATE POST CODE

Ship to:
Acme Gremlins Ltd
Unit 567, Superb Industrial Park
EXPERTVILLE
STATE POST CODE

Attention: Ms Lynda Davies	**INVOICE NO:** 000054398
Customer PO No: TH4513	**Date:** 27 August 2019

Special instructions: 1. Keep widget boxes upright
2. Needs a signature on receipt

Quantity	Item code	Description	Unit price	Total
100	AF63	Widgets – green laminate	0.93	93.00
300	AF97	Widgets – brass	0.99	297.00
1	CD794	Machine to turn widgets	657.00	657.00
1	TR03	3-hour training course on site on 19 August Participants: Grace Shearer and Michael Mitchell	350.00	350.00
1	SVE004	Service call out 24 August 2018	120.00	120.00
			Sub total	**$1,517.00**
			GST @ 10%	**$151.70**
			Total	**$1,668.70**

Thank you for choosing *Table Top Widgets Plc*

Terms of trade: 30 days from date of invoice
Payment due date: 27 September 2019

A query? If you have a query regarding this invoice, please call Ann Jones on 03 6932 9485.
Ann is your accounts contact and will be happy to help you.

Cheques made payable to:
Table Top Widgets PLC

Post to:
PO Box 7395
GRACEVILLE
STATE POSTCODE

Pay direct to:
Best West Bank Pty Ltd
Account name: Table Top Widgets PLC
BSB: 783-962
Account number 834-984-742

IMPORTANT: Please quote our invoice number with your payment

www.tabletopwidgets.com
ACN 000 710 371 190
Table Top Widgets Plc is licenced under the Widget Agreement: Licence Number 000439-571

12. THE BEST WAY TO SEND INVOICES TO GET PAID FAST: EMAIL

'A lack of clarity could put the brakes
on any journey to success.'

*Steve Maraboli, bestselling author, behavioural scientist
and motivational speaker*

Now you have your perfect invoices ready, it's time to get them to your customers as fast as possible. The quicker they are in the right hands, the quicker they'll be paid.

If you don't already send invoices by email (or email them from your accounting software), it's a good idea to start doing so because they arrive instantly. No more postal delays.

Email is very effective, just so long as the email is easy for your customer to read, and so they can see all the pieces of information they need to authorise your invoice for payment. You can usually send emails direct from your accounting software, which makes life easier.

By using the subject line to your advantage, you can make it very clear what is attached to your email. For example, if it's just one invoice, give all the details in the subject line. Then include a brief note in the email and address it to a specific person. This is shown in the following example.

Invoice #14325, dated 1 December 2018, value $7450 attached

Hello Charles,

Please find attached here the above invoice, which is due for payment on 31 December 2018.

If you are unable to download the invoice or you have any queries relating to it, please call me on (XX) XXXX XXXX. I will be happy to answer any queries or questions you may have.

With best regards,

Jan Reeves

If you are sending several invoices at the same time, you can be clear in a slightly different way: in the subject line, include the total of the invoices. This is shown in the following example.

Four invoices for December 2018, total $8944.57

Hello James,

Please find attached here the invoices relating to the above:

01/09/2018 Inv. No 5847	$2556.97
05/09/2018 Inv. No 6492	$2654.63
17/09/2018 Inv. No 7129	$1976.54
23/09/2018 Inv. No 7910	$1756.43
	————
Total	$8944.57

These invoices are due for payment by 31 December.

If you're unable to download the invoices, or have any other query, please call me immediately on (XX) XXXX XXXX, and I'll be happy to help.

With best regards,

Jan Reeves

Invoices are the most valuable documents in your business. Managing invoices so that they get to the customer and the customer pays them on time is as important as making a sale.

If your invoices are not received and actioned by the right person, you run the risk of your invoice not being paid by the due date.

If you have too many invoices that are paid late, your cashflow could dry up altogether.

Just imagine what would happen if you didn't send invoices out at all. It wouldn't be long before you went out of business. Too many overdue invoices can have the same effect.

Emailing invoices to customers gives you the opportunity to send it directly to the person who is authorised to verify it, sign it off for payment or arrange to make the payment.

In my business quite a few of our customers were big 'household name' companies, and several different people were involved with our invoices – for example:

- the Line Manager who placed the order (our point of contact all through fulfilment of the order)

- the Human Resources Manager, who had to be consulted by the Line Manager before he placed the order

- the Accounts Payable department who had to 'log' the invoice into the system, and then send back to the Line Manager for approval

- the Human Resources Manager for a counter-signature who then had to send it back to Accounts Payable to facilitate the payment to us.

One time we got into an enormous mess with invoices to a large telecommunications company. We had been sending our invoices to the Line Manager, as the work we'd done related to his department.

At that stage I hadn't devised this five-step system so we hadn't made a service call to find out to whom and where our invoices needed to go; we'd just sent them to the Line Manager because we had been doing the work for him.

Line Managers have their own job to do and, as we learnt, generally speaking, they aren't responsible for paying invoices. Certainly paying invoices wasn't part of this Line Manager's responsibilities which we discovered when we realised that our invoices hadn't been paid and called to find out what the problem was. He was very apologetic but he thought they were just copies for his reference.

We learnt from that experience that if we didn't ask a company exactly who to send the invoices to and exactly what names needed to be on them … well, we just wouldn't get paid. That's when we started to *set our business up for collections success*.

* * *

Now that you know how to write a 'killer' invoice to make it easy for your customer to pay on time, the next step is to make sure you are fully prepared before you contact a customer about an invoice, so that you can feel 100% confident asking for payment.

KEY POINTS

- Invoices are the most valuable documents in your business. Getting them to your customer quickly so your customer can pay on time is as important as making a sale.

- Emailed invoices get to your customer the same day. The sooner the customer has them, the sooner they can pay.

- The clearer your invoices are, the quicker your customer can see what they need to do and are more likely to take action rather than put them on 'a pile for later'.

TO DO

1 Create your invoices as soon as the work is done and email them to your customer – the same day.

2 Email the invoice to a specific person who knows to expect it.

3 Use the subject line wisely in your emails. Include all the invoice details.

4 Re-read your emails before you send them and try to cut down the text by half to make them succinct and super-clear.

13. INVOICING AND GETTING PAID; LARGE MULTINATIONALS AND UTILITIES VS SMEs VS MICROBUSINESSES

WHY LARGE COMPANIES OFTEN DON'T PAY SMALL BUSINESSES

Invoicing and getting paid via different-sized companies and businesses need completely different strategies.

Large and multinational organisations (for example, household names like Coca-Cola, Toshiba, Unilever, Johnson & Johnson) and utility companies (often called non-commercial or government) generally have a great many employees in each department.

To make the business run smoothly, they will have a great many systems and procedures. They will almost certainly have a step-by-step system for paying invoices, and each organisation's system will be unique to them. For example:

- They will almost always need to see an order number on the invoice, so they can match up an order with an invoice before they can pay it.

- You might be lucky and have just one person in the Accounts Payable department dealing with your account and invoices, but in a large organisation there might be several. Getting to know how a customer's payment system works is really important.

This is even more crucial in shared service centres.

Shared service centres (including 'on-shoring' and 'off-shoring')

You might have heard these terms if you supply to large organisations. This is probably one of the biggest areas of payment challenge for small business owners and is often why big companies are labelled as 'slow payers'. It's not because they don't want to pay, it's because invoices have to comply with their system to get paid.

Here's how it works. Any large organisation might move a section of their business overseas to save on wage costs. The accounting function is one of the first departments to move because there are highly skilled accounting staff, where the cost of living and good wages are a lot less, for example the Philippines and India.

This model works by having documented, standardised processes. Numerous 'work instructions' are written up and the team members are trained to follow the work instructions.

Consequently, any issues that don't conform to the standardised work instructions or any customer query that is a little complex will get held up or go around and around in circles because there's no work instruction that fits.

The key is to make sure that your invoices are correct, and also taking the time to understand your customers' 'order to cash process' and what is required for payment.

At a basic level, this will almost certainly involve ensuring invoices match purchase orders from a price, quantity and even format perspective. Some organisations will not even be able to pay an invoice if the invoice line items are in a different order to the purchase order.

Goods or services will need to be receipted electronically in the computerised accounting system, so they get flagged 'okay to pay'.

In reality, if you are dealing with a shared service centre, you will have to understand their processes better than they do to make sure all the boxes are ticked along the way, so they can just push a button to pay you (because that's what they do).

Because these departments are large, you will often not speak to the same person twice or sometimes not be able to speak with anyone at all, so the next key is to understand the escalation path as there will always be a representative in the 'home' country who is responsible for the team's work. It is these people who will receive the escalated calls when suppliers don't get paid and may have stopped supplying.

If you sell to a customer who has a shared service accounting function, you must get to understand this process and the people involved to make absolutely sure your invoices will flow through their system quickly so you get paid.

GETTING PAID BY AN SME

This can be a much easier process but will still have its own challenges. SMEs are generally considered to have fewer than 250 employees so you'll find a lot of variation in the way each one sets up and structures their accounts departments and invoice payment procedures.

As an example, my company was on the smaller end of the scale and had 28 employees. I had a finance manager who looked after all the accounting, and reporting to her was a part-time administrator who looked after only our invoice payments (accounts receivable). With just 28 employees it was easy for customers to know the name of our administrator (and the finance manager and me).

Almost certainly, in companies between 5 and 250 employees there will be at least one person dedicated to accounts receivable, and that person will work either 'in-house' – usually on the business premises – or the accounts receivable process can still be outsourced in the home country or overseas. It's still paramount to get your invoices right and know the 'order to cash process' in your SME customers.

GETTING PAID BY A MICRO BUSINESS

A micro business is a 'one-man band' and it's the owner (or sometimes the owner's partner or an external bookkeeper) who will know everything about what is going on in their business and will be your contact.

KEY POINTS

- Invoicing and getting paid via different-sized companies and businesses need different strategies.

- Big organisations are often labelled as 'slow payers'. If they pay slowly, generally it's not because they don't want to pay, but because the invoice hasn't complied with their process and consequently has been held up.

- Any large organisation will have a step-by-step automatic or semi-automatic process for paying invoices. Accounts departments can be huge with many people involved in the invoice approval and payment process.

- You need to know how their process works and what you need to do to make sure your invoice flows smoothly through their system and gets paid.

TO DO

1   Make a list of the five largest commercial and non-commercial organisations where you have difficulty getting your invoices paid on time.

2   Ask yourself the following questions on each of the five:

- How much do I know about how this organisation approves and pays invoices?

- Who do I need to contact to get to understand their process?

- What changes do we need to make to ensure our invoices flow through their system?

- If there is a hold up in the future, who do I need to speak to? Who will be able to help me resolve this issue?

Step 2

HOW TO FEEL 100% CONFIDENT ASKING FOR PAYMENT

We've seen in the previous chapters that the best and least confronting way to get invoices paid is to engage your customers and build a positive working relationship with them throughout the sales process. When you do that, customers grow to value your service, like you and *want* to pay you on time. Providing great customer service has the added benefit of customers liking you and preferring to work with you, rather than your competition, and so you keep your valuable customers for the long term.

Now you are talking to customers in the positive environments of 'setting them up for success' and 'killer' invoices, your confidence around speaking to customers will have already grown. Step 2 has some more strategies to add to your confidence to further develop trust and a strong business relationship with your customers.

14. HOW TO FEEL 100% CONFIDENT WHEN TALKING TO CUSTOMERS

'Knowledge is power.'

Francis Bacon (1561–1626), English philosopher,
statesman, scientist and author

So far you have learned that getting invoices paid by the due date is just a matter of following a proven customer service strategy that provides outstanding service to customers by:

- setting customers up for payment success

- sending out only killer invoices – the 100% correct invoices that make excuses not to pay vanish

- getting people to like you and trust you

- focusing on customer satisfaction.

In this chapter we look at some easy strategies you can use to feel 100% confident about asking for payment of your invoices.

KNOWLEDGE IS POWER

To feel 100% confident when talking to your customers actually all you need is a little knowledge.

Learning about the customer's background with your business and learning to take 'collections shorthand' will be a great help. Let's have a look at each of these.

'Insecurity exists in the absence of knowledge.'

Anon

Knowledge = Power   Power = Confidence

The power of background knowledge

To provide great service, you need a little background knowledge about your customer's previous work history including details of all their current invoices and any other items on the account. If you have access to your customer's order number, and what's on the invoice, that's even more knowledge, so more power. Then, whatever they ask you about their account, you will be familiar with.

If you don't currently have easy access to this information when you make a call, it's something worth working towards, because when you are speaking to your customer, having knowledge will make you feel powerful, and knowledge and power equal confidence.

Ideally, you'll have all the details on your computer screen, or maybe a detailed printout of your customer's account. This way, you can be well prepared for any questions your customer might ask.

Here's an example of a checklist you can run through before you make your call so you feel prepared.

Checklist before calling a customer for payment:

1   Check customer file for any known queries.

2   Check with colleagues for any known queries.

3   Check the order details with the invoice to make sure they match.

4   Read any notes about previous conversations with the customer.

5   Have a list of all account transactions in front of you (e.g. invoice and credit note details).

6   Have 'If you don't know the answer' dialogue handy (explained later in this chapter).

7   Remind yourself that the customer has ordered and received the goods or service and does expect to have to pay.

8   Remind yourself that there may be a legitimate reason for non-payment.

9   Use your best customer service skills to build rapport with your customer.

Collections 'shorthand'

The second tip that will give you confidence is called 'collections shorthand'.

WRITE UP NOTES TO JOG YOUR MEMORY

Record conversations and agreements

Learning some 'collections shorthand' will help you feel confident in your calls with your customers. Collections shorthand allows you to make some quick notes during your conversation, which you can then have easy access to, to jog your memory the next time you speak to your customer. You can quickly glance through those notes before you chat with them next time.

Here are some examples of 'collections shorthand' I've used after speaking with a customer. You can adapt them to suit yourself, or they might give you an idea of how to develop your own.

Adv will sp to mktg mger. *Dely not complete.*	Advised I will speak to Marketing Manager – he says delivery not complete.
Called x 3. 3/3.30 & 4pm *no an ea time.*	Called three times at 3 pm, 3.30 pm and 4 pm – no answer each time.
Evy time I call ph *engaged.*	Every time I call the phone is engaged.

Price diff on inv 568: we charged $4 b4 – why now $6? Query to Simon 4/5. In diary to f/up 6/5.	There's a price difference on invoice 568. We charged $4 last time and $6 this time. Query sent to Simon 4 May. Diary to follow up 6 May.
Diff conv.	Difficult conversation.
Asked sev Qs.	Asked several questions.
All Dec inv pment run Fri bar 3756.	All December invoices in their payment run on Friday except invoice 3756.

HOW TO KNOW THE ANSWER TO EVERY QUESTION

'Confidence is a habit that can be developed by acting
as if you already had the confidence you desire to have.'

Brian Tracy, motivational speaker and self-development author

Even with all my preparation, I once felt completely at a loss when a customer asked me how we had resolved a tricky problem on the previous month's invoice. I was totally caught off guard.

I could tell that it was important to the customer, and although I had been involved I actually couldn't remember the specifics about the incident. I didn't like the feeling of being 'lost for words', and I felt all my confidence draining away. After that incident, I developed a strategy so that no-one in my business ever felt 'lost for words' when speaking to a customer again. We could all feel confident, even when we didn't know the answer.

Having knowledge helps you feel confident but there will always be times when we don't have the knowledge to answer a customer's question. I developed the following strategy to help us all feel confident even if we didn't know an answer.

This strategy is sometimes called:

'Fake it till you make it.'

And this is how it works. When you're not sure of the answer to any question, say, completely honestly:

'I'm sorry, I'm not 100% positive on that. Let me find out and come back to you straight away. I'll call you before 12:00 today.'

There's nothing wrong with admitting you don't know something. It's much better than giving somebody incorrect information and it's great customer service to commit to a time to call back. Even if you haven't been able to find the answer, just call back to let your customer know what you've done so far, and when they can expect to hear from you again.

Here's some more examples:

'I'm not sure about that John. Let me find out and get back to you later this morning. Will you be there around 11 am, or what time would suit you better?'

'I'm not 100% positive on that issue. Let me find out and come back to you straight away. Will you still be there in an hour?'

'I'm sorry; I just don't have the answer to that on hand. Will you hang on for 10 seconds please while I ask my colleague?'

'I've heard the Warehouse Manager talk about that; though I'm not sure what the outcome was. I'll run down and see him now and call you right back. Are you going out in the next 30 minutes or so?'

'I think that's right, but I'd like to check so I give you a 100% correct answer. Will you hold on while I ask the Accountant, please? She's just two desks away.'

YOU DON'T HAVE TO KNOW EVERYTHING

Don't know the answer? It's OK!
✓ Arrange a call-back time

Being honest and offering to find an answer as soon as possible is great customer service which is rare, and your customers will appreciate it and remember it. This is just another way to get your customers to like you so they pay you on time.

In the next chapter we will look at what to do (and not do) to develop trust with customers to strengthen your business relationships so you gain even more confidence.

KEY POINTS

- Knowledge is power, so being fully informed and being prepared is important. If you have easy access to previous transactions and conversations with your customer when you talk with them you'll feel relaxed and confident.

- No-one knows the answer to everything. Have a couple of sentences handy that you can use to make your customer feel special and valued until you find the answer and get back to them.

- Think of getting back to your customer with the answer as another opportunity to get them to value your service and like you.

TO DO

1   Decide now how you will make your notes so you can easily refer to them before you next speak to your customer.

2   Decide which two of the example sentences you think you would use the most.

3   Make a note of the examples you'd use and put them where you can easily see them. You'll be prepared when a customer next asks you a question you don't know the answer to.

15. TELEPHONE MASTERY – WORLD CLASS TACTICS

'Be prepared.'

*Robert Baden-Powell, writer and founder of
the Boy Scouts and Girl Guides*

THE BOY SCOUT APPROACH: HOW TO PREPARE BEFORE MAKING A CALL

We saw in the previous chapter that to feel confident you need to be armed with some of your customer's history. Knowledge gives you confidence.

Earlier in the book I explained how important it is to give your customer good service to try to build a positive relationship with them. If building relationships with customers is a new concept for you, take two minutes beforehand to prepare so that you get what you want out of the call.

For example, you can ask yourself one of these questions:

- 'How can I approach this call today, so I leave a great impression on this customer?'

- 'What do I need to do today to build stronger business relationships with my customers?'

- 'When I talk to a customer today and they have a query on an invoice, what do I need to say so they think my service is outstanding?'

- 'What can I do or say in this call today that will encourage this customer to like me?'

- 'What can I do or say in this call to make this customer think I'm awesome?'

Later in this chapter I share some of the ways I've started a 'relationship building' conversation with a customer around invoices.

SUPERHERO TIPS FOR MAKING OR RECEIVING A CALL

In my business, because we wanted customers to like us, *want* to pay our invoices on time, give us more orders and refer us to their business-owner friends, we wanted to give them the very best experience in all their interactions with us, and so together we developed this set of guidelines for making or receiving a call:

- Let the phone ring several times before answering – otherwise the caller isn't prepared. (Three rings is good.)

- The phone is our 'front line'. The impression we give when answering the phone will be a lasting one. It must be a good one.

- Customers take much more notice of the tone of our voice (75%) than the words we say (25%). See more about this in chapter 24.

- 'Welcome to [The Name of Our Company], this is [Your Name]' is the best telephone greeting. The last word spoken is the one remembered.

- If the staff member the customer asks for is out, away from their desk or on the phone, use one of these responses:

  - '...is out of the office until [time they are expected back].'

- – '…is away from his/her desk.'
- – '…is on another call.'

This is followed by, 'Can I or anyone else help you?'

- We are always polite and helpful and we smile while talking on the phone – it creates an impression of interest and friendliness.

- When taking messages, we repeat their phone number and write down what the caller is saying. It can be very useful later.

- We are always professional and use positive language like:
  - – 'Thanks for holding.'
  - – 'Yes, certainly.'
  - – 'It's a pleasure.'

- We avoid using negative words and phrases like:
  - – 'Not bad.'
  - – 'Not a problem.'
  - – 'Sorry to keep you waiting.'

- We acknowledge the caller; that is, 'Hi Sandra, this is Stephen. How can I help you?'

- Be aware of over-familiarity; for example, don't use 'mate' or 'darling' or similar – even if they do.

- Don't ask, 'How are you?' if you don't know the person. Try, 'It's good to speak to you,' or, 'How can I help you?'

- Concentrate on the conversation if you are writing or typing at the same time.

- If you put a caller on hold, explain why and how long you will be.

- When you are out of the office, tell reception how long you will be and what you would like them to tell callers.

- Return all calls – if you can't, find someone who can.

- Not sure of the answer? Just say, 'I'm sorry, I'm just not sure. Can I find out and come back to you?' No-one will object.

- When a customer finishes a conversation with you, they should feel that you have been helpful.

- Best practice is to hang up after the caller has.

- Have a call objective. Prepare a script. Know what you want to say and what you want to get out of the call.

- Have a greeting and reason for calling: 'Good morning, this is Jan Reeves from Get Paid! I need to talk to you about...'

- Speak clearly. Taking the time to speak clearly and in a positive, professional tone will put the caller at ease.

- Hear, listen and understand. Listen carefully to customers and let them finish without interrupting.

6 EASY WAYS TO CONFIDENTLY START A CONVERSATION WITH A CUSTOMER

When calling customers about invoices, it's a good idea to start with an icebreaker, something positive and topical. For example:

'Good morning Charles. How is the office move going? Are you all organised and tidy again? That's excellent.'

'Hello Mary – thanks for taking my call. How's your weather there today? We've got rain here, but all's good – we need it!'

'Hi Mary – Jan Reeves here from Get Paid! We haven't spoken before but I'm the one who looks after your account. Good to finally get to talk to you. Have you been with ABC Renovations for a long time?'

'Hi Mary – it's Jan Reeves here from Get Paid! I'm just calling to introduce myself and give you my direct line in case you ever

have a question about one of our invoices and you need to get hold of me.'

'Hi John – thanks for including payment of that old invoice in your last cheque run. It's so good to get your account up to date. It's looking pretty clear now.'

'Good morning Charles. I thought I'd give you a call and let you know my direct number, so that if you ever have a query about any of our invoices, you can get on to me straight away. I'll sort it out for you for sure.'

KEY POINTS

- Decide what you want to get out of a call before you make one and prepare what you will say.

- When customers like your service, they get to like you too. They are also more likely to pay you on time. Proven.

TO DO

1   Develop your own set of guidelines for making or receiving a call to give your customers the best impression of you and your business.

2   Start a conversation with your customer with a positive icebreaker.

16. HOW TO GET CUSTOMERS TO PAY YOU FIRST

Building a strong working relationship with my customers and getting them to like me was one of the very first strategies I learned when I started to collect payments. I learnt it over 40 years ago from Norman May, who at the time was the credit manager of Gulton Europe, and my boss.

When I went to work for Norman, I didn't feel confident at all about asking customers to pay. Norman explained to me that most people are pleasant, most people want to be helpful, and most people want to do a good job, so I should just try to build a connection with them.

Following Norman's tutelage, I learned to approach people with a friendly, helpful, service-oriented attitude, and very soon I enjoyed talking to customers, and I could tell they enjoyed talking to me too. Together, we sorted out any problems preventing payment. We built great, mutually beneficial working relationships.

Providing great service to customers is a really satisfying way to work and I enjoyed my job. Customers were very appreciative of my customer service and 'can-do' attitude. And when I had to ask them to do something, like pay our invoice on time, they were happy to.

'Kind words do not cost much yet they accomplish much.'

Blaise Pascal, physicist, mathematician,
inventor and writer

* * *

The strategies in Step 2 should have added to your confidence levels. In Step 3 I share my unbeatable 'insider secret' – the ultimate winning strategy to getting invoices paid on time.

KEY POINT

Give your customer your undivided attention while you are talking to them and treat them with courtesy and respect. They will feel important and valued, they'll appreciate your good service, and like you for it.

TO DO

What could you *stop* doing and *start* doing so your customers feel more valued and get to like you more?

- I can stop…(list five things)
- I can start…(list five things)

THE 'INSIDER SECRET' AND HOW TO MINIMISE PROBLEMS THAT CAUSE PAYMENT DELAYS

Now that you know how important it is to build a friendly, positive business relationship with your customers (because people *pay* people they like), and you know how to prepare and send an invoice so that your customer can easily pay it, it's time to discover the real 'insider secret' to getting paid on time. This insider secret is what I call 'the courtesy call'.

If I could give you just one strategy that will improve your collections results and cashflow, it would be the courtesy call. The courtesy call is a champion. Not many people know about it, and you'll soon see how using this simple strategy will put you far ahead of your competition.

The courtesy call is a customer service call made *before* payment is due, and it's designed to make the caller look like a customer service superhero.

Now that you know how to create a 'killer' invoice, it should be error-free and with the right person in the right place. The objective of the courtesy call is to find out, before the invoice is due for payment, if there's a problem somewhere that has 'slipped through the net' and that might delay your invoice being paid. When you remove any last remaining problems on an invoice before the payment due date, you're in the perfect position to get paid on time.

If you wait until after the due date, when your payment hasn't arrived, and then find out there's a problem, your invoice is already overdue. By the time you've resolved the query, your payment can be several weeks late.

The courtesy call minimises (annihilates, almost) problems that cause payment delays. It makes you look like a caring customer service superhero and your business look like a customer service champion.

17. PLANNING YOUR 'COURTESY CALL'

'Fail to plan, plan to fail.'

Mark Twain, writer, entrepreneur, publisher and humourist

In my business, we found it was worthwhile to take a minute to plan our courtesy calls, so that we achieved exactly the outcome we wanted. That outcome was to find out *before* the invoice was due for payment if there was a problem somewhere that would hold up our payment. If we did uncover a problem we could then fix it super-fast with our best customer service. Customers just love great service, so by making courtesy calls our customers came to like us, trust us, pay us on time, and reorder as well.

> Always plan and prepare for your courtesy
> calls before picking up the phone.

We learnt that one way to get customers to like us was to be (and sound) interested in their company. One way we did this was to take the 'knowledge is power' approach, so before we spoke to them we quickly made sure we were aware of all their orders and invoices, and any current working arrangements that we had with them.

Taking an interest in your customer's company is important, regardless of if they are the owner or an employee. If you find out a little bit about their business, you'll have something that you can refer to when you speak to them. Your customer will feel important and feel that you care.

**CUSTOMERS JUST THINK
YOU'RE AWESOME!**

The Courtesy Call
SERVICE   SERVICE   SERVICE
HOT HOT HOT
Customer Likes You,
Trusts You and Pays You!

As your customers get to like and trust you, they will be much more likely to pay your invoices before other suppliers' invoices, and by the due date. Prepare for your courtesy call so you show a genuine interest in the person you are speaking to and their business.

In the next chapter I show you how, if we did uncover a problem that might hold up payment of our invoice, we resolved it as quickly as we could – instantly if possible. That way we put our customer in the position where they had *no reason not to pay* our invoice on time.

KEY POINTS

- Plan and prepare for your courtesy calls before picking up the phone.

- Take the 'knowledge is power' approach. Have some background knowledge of your customer and current transactions with you.

- Show interest in your customer and their business and they'll be interested in you and your business.

- When people are interested in you they are more likely to help you (including by paying your invoice first).

TO DO

What two questions could you ask your contact in your biggest three customers to help you understand their business better?

18. THE COURTESY CALL

'Just try new things. Don't be afraid.
Step out of your comfort zone and soar.'

Michelle Obama, former First Lady of the United States

The courtesy call is a *customer service* call, *not* a *collections* call.

We all want to avoid making collections calls because they are such a negative interaction with a valued customer. The 'courtesy call' is an integral part of the simple five-step system I designed to make sure our customers paid on time, so we *avoided having to make collection calls*.

The 'courtesy call' is the real secret to payment success.

We used this call for 15 years in my small business. We made this 'courtesy call' not to ask for payment of an invoice (but it did get the invoice paid on time), we made it to make our customers feel valued and important with outstanding customer service.

The courtesy call is a really exciting and successful strategy. Not many people know how to do it, so using it in your business will put you well ahead of your competition: you'll get paid on time and customers will think of you as a superhero.

> The courtesy call will turn you into a
> customer service superhero.

HOW A COURTESY CALL WORKS

For this example, we'll use an invoice with terms of '30 days from invoice date'.

We made the 'courtesy call' 10 to 14 days after the customer had received our invoice, under the guise of making sure they were completely satisfied.

> **Invoice dated 1 June ➜ Courtesy call 10–14 June**
> **➜ Payment due date 30 June**

We made our 'courtesy call' to ask our customer, 'Is everything okay?'

Because hardly any supplier ever calls a customer just to ask, 'Is everything okay', we got to look like customer service superheros. And because we spoke to our customers more often, they got to know us well (and much better than any of our competitors).

Our customers loved the great service we were providing. And as they got to know us and trust us they went out of their way put our invoices to the front of their payment queue so we got paid on time

This strategy worked brilliantly for my small business. We got our invoices paid on time and saved ourselves heaps of time and frustration not having to follow up unpaid invoices. And we had the added benefits of having customers that liked and trusted us, who gave us repeat orders and referred us to other potential customers too.

If you are already setting customers up for payment success and following the 'killer' invoice strategy, your invoice should have all the information that your customer needs to be able to approve and pay the invoice. If that's the case, you still get the chance to look like a caring customer service hero just because you've asked, 'Is everything okay'? But, even after employing all the tips in Step 1, you still might find instances where your customer has a query and the invoice might need an adjustment.

Any invoice that needs an adjustment isn't going to be paid. By using the courtesy call strategy, we got to know *before* the invoice was due for payment if there was something that might prevent it being paid on time. This is when the courtesy call becomes really valuable. Using your outstanding customer service skills you can immediately take control and resolve the issue super-fast so that they *can* pay.

You can apologise that something 'isn't quite right', tell them 'not to worry at all', and that you will 'personally resolve this for them'. Just imagine how important and valuable that will make your customers feel.

RESOLVE INVOICE ISSUES QUICKLY AND STILL GET PAID ON TIME

We learnt to resolve queries quickly for two reasons:

1 It gave us a chance to get to know our customers better while we were resolving the query. The better the relationship, the easier it is to get an invoice paid.

2 All the time there was a query on the invoice, the customer wouldn't be paying it, so it was in our interests to sort it out quickly.

Often, we would try to sort out a query the same day – sometimes we would ask the customer to 'hold on for a moment, let me see if I can sort this out for you right away'.

Mostly, we explained what we would need to do to resolve the query and asked when would be a convenient time later that day to call them back with the outcome.

Even if we weren't able to resolve the query by the designated time, we always called the customer back to give them an update and made another time to call again with the answer.

Calling to find out if a customer has a problem with an invoice *before* the due date works brilliantly and will help you get paid.

HOW TO SECURE YOUR PAYMENT DURING THE COURTESY CALL

At the end of the courtesy call, you have the chance to actually ask for your payment. This is another opportunity for you to uncover any further issues that may hold up the invoice. Here are some ways to do this:

'Gosh! Mary, sorting out those prices was all a bit of a challenge, wasn't it? I'm so pleased we were able to sort that out quickly for you. Now that the invoice is cleared for payment, is there

anything stopping it from being included in your payment run on Friday?'

'Thanks for being so patient with those queries, Mary. It's great when our customers are "on our side". I really appreciate it. Now that the invoice is correct, I can see it's actually due for payment tomorrow. When is your next scheduled payment run? Do you think you might be able to include it?'

'Oh, that's a shame – although we've sorted out that query for you now, we've missed this payment run and the next one is in two weeks. What chance do I have, if I ask you really nicely, to organise a special payment for us in the next couple of days for these three invoices?'

In the next chapter you will learn how we used the courtesy call to resolve any issues delaying payment and still get paid on time.

KEY POINTS

- The courtesy call is *a customer service call* made *before* the invoice is due for payment to find out if there's a problem that might prevent the invoice being paid on time.

- When you remove all and any problems before the due date, you can put yourself in a position to ask for payment on time. While doing that, you can work on building your friendly and helpful relationship with the client.

- If you wait until *after* the due date and then call your customer to chase up your payment, and then find out there's a problem, the invoice is already overdue. By the time the query is resolved, the payment can be several weeks late.

- Building on the strategy 'if people like you, they pay you,' the courtesy call gives the customer such outstanding helpful service that they will think you are a customer service superhero!

TO DO

Which three existing customers would you like to pay you earlier? Prepare what you are going to say, and then make a courtesy call to each one. Find out if there are any errors preventing payment of your invoices, and use your great customer service attitude to build your friendly, professional relationship.

19. HOW TO BREAK THE ICE

'Every action needs to be prompted by a motive.'

*Leonardo da Vinci (1452–1519), mathematician,
painter, sculptor, architect*

HOW TO PUT CUSTOMERS AT EASE: START WITH AN 'ICE BREAKER'

You might have heard the old saying, *'You catch more bees with honey than vinegar'*.

And another old saying: *'What you give out, you get back.'*

Well, they've both been in use for a long, long time – because they've both been proven to be true. The more pleasant and helpful you are, the more people will like you, and they'll treat you in the same way you treat them.

Get customers to like you by providing great service and quickly solving any queries or problems they have. Use every opportunity you can to build a positive business relationship with your customers.

When you call your customers, start your conversation with an icebreaker. Ask a positive and topical question rather than launching straight into a conversation asking about your invoices.

PUT YOUR CUSTOMER AT EASE

✓ Break the ice
✓ Be friendly and engaging
✓ Positive and professional
✓ Genuinely complimentary
✓ Say thanks

For example, if you already know your customer, you might say something like this:

'Hi, Bob. Thanks for taking my call. It's always great to speak to you. You always sound so happy and positive when you answer the phone.'

Or you could say:

'Good morning Charles. It might look as if I'm stalking you, but I promise I'm not. I just thought I'd call you again to let you know that I've raised that credit for the six broken widgets. It comes to $96.60. So, I thought I'd call and let you know, just because I know you were keen to resolve that issue. Should I email it to you now?'

HOW TO RESOLVE ISSUES DELAYING PAYMENT AND STILL GET PAID ON TIME

Occasionally, invoice errors or problems will occur even after 'setting customers up for success' and using 'killer' invoices. When you make your courtesy call, if your customer can't pay an invoice, it is generally for one of two reasons:

- **There's something wrong with the invoice or the goods.** This is usually easy to fix. Something like a costing issue or a proof of delivery might be needed, and the invoice will be paid when that's supplied.

- **Your customer is short of money.** If that's the case, you get to know about it early because you made your courtesy call.

> Sometimes customers don't pay because they simply don't have the money.

If your customer raises a query with the invoice or goods and you are investigating that for them, let them know:

- what you will do

- when you will do it

- when you will get back to them (even if you haven't solved the problem yet and can only give them an update).

It's very professional (and great customer service) to commit yourself to a timeframe to get back to your customer.

Here are some examples of what to say. You can adapt them to suit your situation:

> 'Oh yes, I can see what's gone wrong here. Could you hold on just one moment while I call David in the warehouse and ask him? I'm sure he'll know the answer and we can sort this out for you right away.'

> 'Let me do that for you Sarah and get back to you straight away. Will you be in your office at 12:00 noon today?'

Or:

> 'I know how to resolve this. I'll just put in a call to Howard and speak to him this afternoon, all being well. In any event, I'll call you back before the close of business today and let you know how my conversation with Howard went and what the next steps are.'

If there is a problem with the invoice, you get the opportunity to use your great customer service skills to solve the problem quickly. When that's resolved to your customer's complete satisfaction, you will have grown your status as a customer service superhero and you'll be in a perfect position to ask your customer if there's any further reason for them not to pay your invoice by the due date. How can they refuse? (We'll address how to handle a customer who is short of money later in the book.)

Now that you know how to 'break the ice' and build strong business relationships with great customer service, in the following chapters you can use those techniques to improve the payment cycle of an existing customer and get new customers off to a 'flying start' by paying on time.

KEY POINTS

- Generally there are two main reasons for non-payment of invoices:

    - There's something wrong with the invoice or the goods.

    - Your customer is short of money.

- The courtesy call will help you find out early if your invoice is likely to be paid on time. If there's a problem you can take appropriate action before the invoice is even due for payment.

- Use a problem on an invoice as an opportunity to use great customer service to solve the problem quickly. Once you've resolved it you will have grown your status as a customer service superhero.

- If you are resolving a query for a customer, let them know: what you will do, when you will do it, and when you will get back to them.

TO DO

Which of your customers is holding up payment of your invoice because of a query? What could you do to quickly and graciously resolve that query today and, by doing that, get your customer to like you so they want to pay your invoice as soon as the query is resolved?

20. IMPROVE PAYMENTS FROM EXISTING CUSTOMERS WITH THE COURTESY CALL

You can use courtesy calls to gradually improve your existing customers' payment times. Start to make all your calls customer-service-focused now, and over a few weeks or months you can gradually bring late-paying customers around to paying on time, every time.

Here's some examples of the type of dialogue we used on customers that had got into the habit of paying late. We just found a reason or an excuse to make a call. These will give you some ideas – you can adapt any of them and find a reason or excuse to call to suit your own current situation:

> *'Hi Jane! This is Jan Reeves here from Get Paid! I thought I'd call you a bit earlier this month. I was a bit concerned that we had made a couple of errors last month and it took a while for us to sort that out for you. Can we just run through this month's invoices now and check that you've got everything you need from us?'*

Or you could say something like:

> 'Hello Jane! This is Jan Reeves here from Get Paid! We've changed our invoicing procedure, so I just thought I'd call to see if everything is correct this month? There are three invoices for this month. Can we run through them now, or is there a better time for you?'

Or another way might be:

> 'Hello, Jane, this is Jan Reeves here from Get Paid! I'm just calling to let you know that we've recently updated our invoice system to cut down on errors. The new system should improve our service, but I thought I'd give you a call anyway just to make sure we've got everything correct on your invoices. Do you have a moment to run through that with me?'

If the answer is no, it's not suitable now, make good use of an 'open question' here:

> 'When will be a good time? When would suit you?'

And then pause to let your customer tell you what time would suit them. Then you can say:

> 'Oh, yes, all right, I'll call you back at two o'clock tomorrow.'

By agreeing on a time, they've given you *an appointment to talk about the invoices.*

KEY POINTS

- The courtesy call is a great way to start to improve payments from your existing customers.

- Make all your calls customer-service-focused from now on. Over time you can gradually bring late-paying customers around to paying on time, every time.

TO DO

1 Make a list of your three biggest customers who consistently pay late. Find a reason or excuse to call them.

2 Decide which of the example dialogues you can adapt to start to get them on the road to paying on time.

21. TRAINING NEW CUSTOMERS TO PAY ON TIME WITH THE COURTESY CALL

The courtesy call works very well when you're just starting to build your business relationship with a new customer. You might say something like:

> *'Jane, hello. It's Jan Reeves from Get Paid! You recently bought some super widgets from us which we delivered last week. That was your first order with us, and we've issued an invoice for $450 to cover that. I'll be looking after your account, so I thought I'd call to introduce myself, make sure I've created your account correctly and that you have everything you need from us. If there's anything you need, I can look after that for you.'*

And then you might ask some questions:

> *'This is how I've set up your account.'*

> *(And then run through all the contact details: name, ship-to address, invoicing address, and so on.)*

> *'Is that all correct? Is there anything else I should add?'*

After you've made any amendments to the account you can ask the invoice questions:

'Do you have that invoice? It's invoice A45674.'

And then pause for them to say 'yes' or 'no'. Then:

'Does the invoice have all the information you need?'

And then pause for them to say 'yes' or 'no', and then you could ask:

'Has it been signed off and authorised for payment yet?'

And pause for them to say 'yes' or 'no'.

Just asking these types of questions from a purely customer-service focus gives you the opportunity to get to know your new customer in a relaxed and friendly way. If the answer is 'yes' that's excellent; if it's 'no' you can quickly take control and resolve the issue that might stop your customer paying the invoice on time, and your client will be thinking, 'What great service this is. These guys are really on the ball.'

In the next chapter we look at how just listening to your customer can help you get paid.

KEY POINTS

- Use the courtesy call to interact with new customers in a positive, helpful way so they see you as a customer service hero from the start of your relationship.

- Quickly and gracefully sort out any queries customers have that may prevent them from paying. They will love the great service, and you'll be building on your customer service hero status.

TO DO

Decide which of the example dialogues you can adapt to get your new customers to pay on time and off to a great start with your business.

22. HOW TO USE YOUR LISTENING SKILLS TO GET YOUR INVOICES PAID

'We have two ears and one mouth.
We need to listen twice as much as we speak.'

Epictetus (50–135 AD), Greek philosopher

START BY ASKING OPEN QUESTIONS

While you're developing your customer service and relationship building skills so your customers get to like you and want to pay you on time, you can add listening skills to your arsenal as well. Just listening can be a powerful way to help you get paid.

Listening skills are often overlooked, but people will tell you just about everything you need to know if you ask the right questions and listen long enough for them to give you the answer. All too often we keep talking, instead of allowing someone to give us the answer that we're looking for.

The types of questions you can ask so you get exactly the answers you want are called 'open' questions. Open questions start with:

> **Who? What? When? Where? How?**

When you need information use these types of questions. Just be careful though, because you'll only get the answer you are looking for if, after you've asked your question, you listen carefully and don't interrupt your customer.

Here's how 'open' questions work. After you ask an open question, pause to give your customer the opportunity to answer. Don't say a word until your customer has answered.

There might be an 'uncomfortable gap' while the customer is thinking – don't be tempted to fill that gap by saying something. If you keep quiet, your customer will close that 'uncomfortable gap' and give you the key piece of information you're looking for.

Here are some examples of the types of questions you could ask, and then pause while the customer thinks and then gives you the answer you want:

- '**What's** the name of the manager who needs to sign off those invoices for payment?' (*Pause.*)

- '**What** do you think I should do to get my invoice paid?' (*Pause.*)

- '**When** is she next expected back in the office?' (*Pause.*)

- '**Who** is looking after that while he's on sick leave?' (*Pause.*)

- '**Where** is his office?' (*Pause.*)

- '**How** will you do that?' (*Pause.*)

OPEN QUESTIONS GET ANSWERS

Ask the right questions + Keep quiet
Get the answer you're looking for

Who? What? When? Where? How?

The Key = PAUSE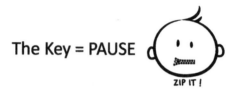

ZIP IT !

HOW TO JUST LISTEN TO GET THE ANSWER YOU WANT

'Listening is so much more important than what you say.'

Hoda Kotb, American broadcaster and journalist

Listening carefully is a simple but powerful strategy to use in any situation where you need an answer. It works brilliantly when you are trying to get invoices paid. It's a super-simple strategy to learn, and once you know how, it's very easy to use.

Customers will give you just about all the information you need if you leave a space for them to answer your question, but people sometimes forget to pause and wait for the answer and instead say something like this:

'I'm calling to speak to John Smith. Is he there today or...'

The 'or' at the end of a question is a bit of superfluous waffle. It sounds as though you aren't clear about the question you are asking. It gives the other person the opportunity to waffle too.

A much more powerful approach is to ask one of those open questions and then simply pause, wait and listen. If you do encounter an 'uncomfortable silence' don't worry, you'll soon get the answer you want. After the little bit of discomfort, you'll feel a sense of achievement.

KEY POINTS

- Asking the right questions and then pausing and listening carefully will almost always get you the answer you're looking for.

- Don't add 'or...' to the end of your questions.

TO DO

1   Every time you think of a question you need a customer to answer, take a minute to reframe your question to make it a powerful 'open' question.

2   Adapt any of the example questions to:

- chase any payments that haven't arrived

- get to speak to the right person

- get through to a person who you think might be trying to avoid you.

Step 4

WHAT TO SAY, WHEN, AND TO WHOM TO GET YOUR INVOICES PAID ON TIME

In Step 4, I explain how *what* you say, *how* you say it and *to whom* you say it can have a huge impact on when customers pay their invoices.

Most small business owners will be like me. I had to get my invoices paid on time, so I could pay my staff, suppliers and myself, and like most business owners, my business would have failed if we hadn't been paid.

Mostly we got invoices paid on time just by using good customer service skills all through the sales process, but from time to time we needed some special strategies for tricky situations. That's what Step 4 is about.

23. IT *IS* WHAT YOU SAY

'That's what careless words do.
They make people love you a little less.'

Arundhati Roy, Indian author and political activist

Every business wants their customers to pay on time, but *we can never force a customer to pay* – that's just not possible. What worked for me was to get people to like me, so *they wanted to pay me.* We all pay people we like first.

During the course of business, there's lots of different reasons to have conversations with your customers. In each instance, your customer needs to feel as if they've had good service. They need to feel well looked after and valued. This is a win/win for everyone. To make sure that I built a positive relationship with every customer I learned to choose my words carefully.

CHOOSING WORDS CAREFULLY: THE SAME THING SAID IN TWO DIFFERENT WAYS

When I was shopping recently, I walked into two businesses and got two different greetings. I felt completely different when I left each one.

In the first one, the shop assistant looked uninterested and shouted at me from the other side of the store:

'Are you right?'

I said that I was 'right' but that I'd like to buy something. She grudgingly put down the labels she had in her hand and walked over. She didn't smile, wasn't helpful, and I left the shop quickly, not buying anything.

I wasn't really surprised at the lack of service (good service is *so* rare), but I did think that it didn't make the future of the business look very promising. With that sort of greeting I wouldn't bother going back to that shop.

The next stop was the bank. I was really surprised by the greeting. The teller greeted me with a wide smile and:

'Hello, how can I help you today?'

I wasn't expecting that. It made me smile too. Already we were off to a good start. As we continued, the teller couldn't have been more helpful and friendly. He answered all my questions in a sunny and positive manner. Being a bank, I wasn't really expecting such a positive experience. I felt uplifted and happy when I left.

GOOD CUSTOMER SERVICE IS RARE

The words we choose when we interact with customers can make a huge difference to how they feel about us.

Good customer service is *rare* so an easy way to stand out from the crowd is to be different and give great service. Even something as simple as saying:

'How can I help you today?'

'Let me do that for you.'

'I'll come back to you with an answer this afternoon.'

'What can I do for you today?'

When someone thanks you for something, you can use one of these (my colleague, Margaret, was expert at this):

'My pleasure.'

'You're welcome.'

'Happy to help.'

Positive language can put your customer – and you – into a positive frame of mind.

KEY POINTS

- Use positive words in conversations with customers. Keep negative words and expressions out of all your conversations. Ditch words and phrases like:

  - not
  - problem
  - can't
  - hardly
  - that's not my job.

- Using the right words is important if you want people to like you (and pay you).

- Positive words are uplifting (for you and your customer).

TO DO

1 Listen to the words and expressions you use daily.

2 Find positive words and expressions to replace any negatives you habitually use.

3 See if you can set up an accountability partnership with someone. Each time you catch yourself or each other using a negative word or phrase, add a small sum of money into a 'negativity' jar and donate the contents to a charity every month.

24. IT IS ALSO DEFINITELY *HOW YOU SAY IT*

'People can be reassured by a tone of voice.'

Jody Shields, editor and author

THE CHALLENGE OF COMMUNICATING OVER THE PHONE

We've learnt through previous chapters that customers are much more likely to pay the suppliers they like first. The challenge is that getting customers to like us over the phone can be a bit difficult, and here's why ...

Face-to-face communications

When we talk to someone face to face, this is how they take in what we say:

- 7% of the time they focus on the *words* that we use.

- 38% of the time they are aware of the *tone* of our voice.

- 55% of the time they are *taking in our body language* and our *facial expressions*.

Over half of how people take in what we say when we talk with them face to face is related to how we are holding our body and the look on our face.

FACE TO FACE COMMUNICATION

7% words

38% tone of voice

55% body language and facial expressions

It's not what we say, it's the way that we say it!

Communicating over the phone

But on the phone, we can't see each other! All we have is our voice and our words. We only have the actual conversation to work with.

This is how people take in what we are saying when we are talking with them on the phone:

- 14% of the time, the customer focuses on the words we use

- 86% of the time, they are taking in the tone of our voice.

So, our voice, and how we use our voice, is by far the most important aspect of getting customers to like us.

THE POWER OF HOW YOU USE YOUR VOICE

The voice has four different parts:

- inflection (tone)
- pitch
- pace
- volume.

Let's look at how each of these affects your phone interactions with your customers.

Inflection

Inflection is the emphasis you put on each word. It's often referred to as 'tone', and it's the way you highlight words or phrases when you are talking.

If you choose carefully, you can use inflection to stress the importance of certain issues, and you can keep your caller engaged and on track. Here's a good example of how you can say the same sentence four times, and by emphasising a different word each time, the sentence takes on four different meanings.

'**I** didn't say I love you.'

'I **DIDN'T** say I love you.'

'I didn't say I **LOVE** you.'

'I didn't say I love **YOU**.'

You can see how by emphasising a word it has a huge impact on the meaning of a conversation we're having.

Pitch

Pitch is how high or how low your voice is, and it affects how people receive your words:

- A **monotone and flat voice** says to your customer, *'I'm bored and have absolutely no interest in what you're talking about'.*

- A **slow speed and low pitch** says, *'I'm depressed and want to be left alone'.*

- A **high pitch and energetic** voice says, *'I'm enthusiastic about this subject'.*

- An **abrupt speed and loud tone** says, *'I'm angry and not open to listening to you'.*

- A **high voice and drawn out speed** says, *'I don't believe what I'm hearing'.*

Pace

Pace is how fast or slow we speak. Whenever we say a person is talking too fast or too slow, we're referring to their pace.

People who talk fast (at a **fast pace**) can get bored if we talk slowly. People with a **slow pace** often don't understand someone who's talking really fast.

When you match a person's pace, they will feel much more comfortable. When someone is comfortable speaking with you, that's another reason for them to like you.

Volume

Mid-range volume works well. Be sensitive to your listener though. Adapt your voice to the volume they are using if you need to.

* * *

Your voice contains elements of **pitch, pace, inflection** and **volume** that make it uniquely yours.

KEY POINTS

- A friendly, business-like tone will make your voice sound confident, helpful and professional.

- Tone is an important element of successful business communications.

- High-pitched voices can sound abrasive, so keep to mid-range. Low, deep voices tend to be much more soothing.

- Keep your pitch mid to low level. Speak slowly and clearly, and adjust your speed to match your customer.

- Volume is probably the easiest element to control. Mid-range is perfect for building relationships with customers.

TO DO

1 Record yourself speaking to your customer (with their permission, for 'training purposes').

2 Play it back and check your inflection, pitch, pace and volume.

3 List three things you can change to give your customer a more positive experience.

25. IT IS ALSO *WHO* AND *HOW* YOU ASK

'Don't bark up the wrong tree.'

English idiom

FINDING THE DECISION MAKERS

When you have an invoice that is overdue, it's easy to explain your problem to the first person you speak to when you contact your customer.

But most people in that business aren't really interested in whether you get paid or not. It's not their problem – they have other responsibilities. So, if you rely on them to relay your message, you can't be sure the message will get to the right person – the person who can make the decision to get your invoice paid. The 'decision maker'.

Who would be the decision maker in a small company?

If it's a micro company, the decision maker could be just the owner (the owner does *everything*). If it's a small company with a few employees, the decision maker might be the owner or their partner.

I CAN GET YOUR INVOICE PAID!

Talk to the DECISION MAKER

Some small businesses have a part-time employee who comes in once or twice a week and some outsource their book keeping or accounting.

Who would be the decision maker in a large organisation?

If it's a larger company, there could be several decision makers:

1 The first decision maker might be the Warehouse Manager. He or she might have to confirm that the delivery was received.

2 It might then go from the Warehouse Manager to a second decision maker, which could be the Accounts Manager who sends the payments.

3 There could also be a Finance Manager who gives the okay for the Accounts Manager to send the payment from the bank.

WHO CAN GET YOUR INVOICE PAID?

FIND THE DECISION MAKER
Who makes all the decisions around here?

When you're chasing an invoice in a large organisation, you might have to chase all three decision makers, one after the other, to get your invoice paid.

How to find your decision maker

Regardless of the size of your customer's company, to find out who the decision maker is, and how to get to speak to them, use an open question (see chapter 22). Those are powerful questions that start with *who? what? when? where?* and *how?*

You might call your customer and say something like this:

'Hello, this is Jan Reeves calling from Get Paid! We sent an invoice through to you recently and I just need to chat to someone about it. Can you tell me who looks after your accounts please?'

Or you might say:

> 'Hello John, this is Jan Reeves calling from Get Paid! I think you have our invoice number 3465 for $3000 on your desk for approval. When will you be approving it and sending it to the accounts department to pay?'

Next time you want to chase an invoice for payment, use open questions to find out who the decision maker is. You're trying to talk to the person who can take the next action to push your invoice towards getting paid.

(Learn more about working with different sized companies in chapter 13.)

PEOPLE WILL TELL YOU JUST ABOUT EVERYTHING YOU WANT TO KNOW IF YOU ASK THE RIGHT QUESTION

Whether you are trying to find the right person to talk to, or you are talking to the right person and you want to know where things are at, these tried-and-tested open questions will help you uncover the exact situation on each of your invoices. Open questions are unbeatable for getting answers:

> '**Who** is it that signs off these invoices for payment?'

> '**When** will she be back?'

> '**What** time will he be back?'

> '**How** will you do that?'

> '**Where** does John work? In your office or another location?'

The key to getting your answer is that you must pause after you've asked your question. Don't say anything. Your customer will feel a little uncomfortable and will 'close the gap' by giving you the answer to the question you have asked.

Once you know the status of each invoice, you're in a position of control. You can quickly resolve any issues preventing payment and when there's no outstanding issues, there's no excuse for your customer not to pay.

Questions to ask to find the 'elusive' person

Asking the receptionist 'open questions' can get you the answers you want.

If you get a situation where the person you want to speak to is always 'out of the office', to find out if they are in the office but avoiding you, ask:

> *'Good morning is Will Brown there today?'* (*Pause and wait*)

(Don't give your name first – just make sure Will is there.)

If he's not, and you're asked if you want to leave a message, just say:

> *'No, thank you. Don't worry about leaving a message for him. I'm just about to make another call – I'll call back.'*

You are keeping control here. There's no point in leaving a message for someone who you think may be trying to avoid you. You can also ask:

> **'What** *time do you think I might catch him?'* (*Pause and wait*)

> **'What** *time do you think I should call back?'* (*Pause and wait*)

> *'Did you say he's on holiday just now?'* (*Pause and wait*) …
> *'Okay, this is why I'm calling* ……… **Who** *is responsible for this in his absence?'* (*Pause and wait*)

Questions to ask to find the the right person to talk to

'Hello, this is Jan Reeves calling from Get Paid! We sent an invoice through to you recently and I just need to chat to someone about it. Can you tell me **who** *looks after your accounts please?' (Pause and wait) …*

'Ah, it's Jane Green is it? Can you put me through to Jane please?' (Pause and wait) …

'Hello Jane, this is Jan Reeves from Get Paid! Jackie on your reception tells me you look after all the accounts – is that right?' (Pause and wait)

If you are told 'this invoice is waiting to be approved', you can ask:

'Who *needs to approve it? Who signs off these invoices for payment?' (Pause and wait)*

This will get you the name of the person you need to speak to next to ask them to approve it. Or you can ask:

'What *is the reason why it hasn't been approved?' (Pause and wait)*

Your contact doesn't know the answer?

'You aren't sure? **Who** *in your company would know that?' (Pause and wait)*

Your contact isn't there?

'Where *are they located?' (Pause and wait)*

'Oh, she's on holiday? **Who** *is responsible in her absence?' (Pause and wait)*

Sticky stuff to sort out?

> 'There's one or two old items on your account that I'd like to run through with you.'

And then use an open question:

> '**When** is a good time?' (Pause and wait)

Pause after asking '**when** is a good time,' and your customer will fill the 'uncomfortable gap' by telling you a time that suits them.

KEY POINTS

- Don't leave messages about your invoices with uninterested parties.

- Speak directly to the decision maker about your invoice – the person who can take action on it.

- Use open questions to:

  - find out how to get hold of the 'elusive' person

  - find out who the decision maker is.

- After asking a question *pause and wait* until your customer answers.

TO DO

1 If you've left messages about your invoices with someone and haven't had a response, adapt one of the example questions to find out who the decision maker is and speak to them.

2 What answers would you like about your five biggest invoices?

3 What open questions can you ask about those five large invoices so you get a definitive answer?

26. HOW TO KEEP CONTROL OF YOUR CONVERSATION (AND YOUR MONEY)

'Clarity is the beginning of a good experience.'

Skip Prichard, CEO of Oberoi Centre of Learning and Development, a global non-profit research organisation

Your outstanding invoices are *your* money. Having an outstanding invoice is just like leaving a pile of your cash with someone. If you want your money back, it's important that you keep control of your invoices even though they're with your customer. You can do that using the powerful **'I'll do, you'll do'** finish at the end of your conversation. That way you'll keep control of both your conversation and your invoices.

HOW TO KEEP CONTROL OF YOUR INVOICES WITH THE 'I'LL DO, YOU'LL DO' FINISH

When you finish a conversation with your customer, if you both need to take an action of some kind you can use this powerful finish to make it clear what needs to happen next and to make sure your customer does their part.

This strategy is a great way to reconfirm what has just been agreed and what needs to be done next to bring the situation to a win/win finish as quickly as possible. It's a win for the customer as they will see they are completely satisfied with the transaction, and a win for you as it moves your invoice nearer to being paid.

This is a tactic that worked well in my business, and I've taught it to lots of other people. Even if you have had a really complicated conversation, this will work brilliantly and allow you to keep control of the conversation and your invoices.

GET COMMITMENT WITH A WINNING FINISH

" I'll do / You'll do" FINISH

"I AM GOING TO..."

"YOU ARE GOING TO..."

"WE'VE AGREED THAT..."

The 'I'll do, you'll do' finish does three things:

- it recaps the conversation

- it reconfirms what you and your customer have agreed to do

- it confirms what will happen next to either bring the issue to a conclusion or take it forward to the next stage.

Here's an example using a query over pricing:

> 'That's marvellous, Charles. So, what I'm going to do is talk to the Sales Manager when he's in the office tomorrow, ask him about that pricing, and then call you tomorrow afternoon. In the meantime, you're going to chat with the purchasing manager just to make sure it had $4.59 per item on the order.'

And the next step is the 'this is the outcome we've agreed' finish, and this is how it goes:

> 'So, when we talk tomorrow afternoon, Charles, if we've got it wrong this end, I'll have that credit note for you, and you'll put it through straight away and include the invoice and credit in your payment run on Friday…Have I got that right? Great. Let's talk tomorrow.'

KEY POINTS

- Think of your outstanding invoices as piles of your cash sitting on your customer's desk. Because that's exactly what they are.

- The 'I'll do, you'll do' finish means you and your customer both finish the call with clarity and a reminder about what steps to take next.

TO DO

1   Make a list of the five biggest overdue invoices you have that are under query with one of your customers, and out of your control.

2   Adapt some of the examples in this chapter and make a plan to chat with your customer and use the 'I'll do, you'll do' finish to regain control.

27. HOW TO MANAGE AN UNHAPPY CUSTOMER (AND AVOID HAVING ONE TO BEGIN WITH)

HOW TO MANAGE AN UNHAPPY CUSTOMER

Not everyone in business is having a nice day today. Sometimes people can be grumpy – and sometimes it can be our fault. When I worked for a big corporation and I asked for payment of an overdue invoice from a customer, I can think of a few times when I was on the receiving end of comments like:

> *'Your Sales Manager said he was going to fix this. We've been overcharged.'*

Ugh... they were really embarrassing situations – and it's not the best customer service image.

I distinctly remember a customer once saying very grumpily to me:

> *'Your Managing Director knows all about this. I suggest you speak to him.'*

To try to diffuse the situation, I tried to make a little bit of a joke (at our MD's expense), and said:

> 'Well … that's no good, you can't rely on anyone these days! Let me apologise on his behalf, Mary. I'll have a chat with him this morning and see if I can resolve that for you today. Will you be there about four o'clock this afternoon?'

By saying I'd take action and call the customer back, I was keeping control of the situation and providing great service at the same time. I was trying to give the customer a better impression of us in the hope of improving her mood.

I couldn't get hold of the MD by 4 pm, so I called the customer back and told her what I'd done, what I was going to do next and when, and when I'd get back to her with an update. I kept liaising with Mary and kept her up to date until I'd completely resolved the situation to her satisfaction. (I was only going to get paid when I'd done that anyhow!)

I kept going with my 'outstanding customer service attitude', and by the time I'd resolved the query, I'd built a great relationship with her. She appreciated what I had done and had grown to like me, so that when I asked her to pay afterwards, she paid immediately.

HOW TO AVOID HAVING UNHAPPY CUSTOMERS

When I started my own business, I really couldn't afford to have an unhappy customer. Happy customers are a pleasure to work with and very valuable. They buy again. Unhappy customers go and buy from the competition.

To avoid unhappy customers, we did several things:

- We listened carefully to what they were ordering and supplied *exactly* (not 'almost') what they wanted.

- We made a point of making them feel welcome, important and valued when interacting with them.

- We 'owned' any query or problem they had and resolved it quickly and with grace.

- We made notes of conversations, so anyone in the company could check the notes and speak to the customer knowledgeably.

It's very expensive to find a new customer, so our strategy paid us back tenfold. Happy customers gave us repeat business and referred us to other potential customers.

KEY POINT

If your company has made a mistake, redeem yourself by owning the problem and providing outstanding service to resolve it quickly. You'll only get paid when the invoice is clear of errors so you might just as well act fast and look like a customer service superhero to increase your chances of getting paid quickly afterwards.

TO DO

1   Think about any customers you have that aren't very happy with you currently.

2   Decide what can you do to provide them with some outstanding service so you look like a customer service superhero and redeem yourself.

28. HOW ASKING FOR HELP CAN HELP YOU GET PAID

'If you light a lamp for somebody,
it will also brighten your path.'

Gautama Buddha, monk and sage

Most people love to help another person. We all feel good when we help someone. So, next time you are trying to speak to someone who is continually 'out of the office', start asking for help.

If you've asked to speak to your contact and the receptionist comes back to you and says, 'He's in a meeting,' you can ask:

'What time will he be free?' (Pause and wait)

Or:

'I really do want to speak to him. What time do you think I should call back?' (Pause and wait)

What you are doing is *asking the receptionist for help*. Because people like to help, the receptionist is quite likely to give you an idea of a time to call back.

The last time I asked that question, the receptionist said, 'I know the meeting will finish at 3:30 as one of the attendees needs to catch a flight'. So, I said:

> *'Oh, thanks! Would you let him know I'm trying to speak with him and that I'll call back at 4 pm?' (Pause and wait)… 'Thanks so much.'*

PEOPLE LOVE TO HELP

Don't be afraid to ask the gatekeeper for help...

Most people really do
LOVE to be helpful

The previous time I asked a similar question, the receptionist gave another helpful hint of how best to catch him. She said:

> *'He's always in the office by 7.30 am. If you call then you're sure to get him. Would you like his direct line?'*

KEY POINTS

- When you ask for someone's help use an 'open' question, then pause and wait for their answer, chances are they'll go out of their way to help you.

- We all love to help other people. It makes *us* feel good when we help someone.

TO DO

1 Which three customers are you currently having difficulty locating and speaking to?

2 Who can you ask to help find them so you can speak to them?

29. CUSTOMER BEING ELUSIVE? HERE'S HOW TO FIND THEM

SIX WAYS TO GET PAST A GATEKEEPER

If you are really having trouble getting hold of the person you need to speak to, try one of these strategies:

1   Ask a colleague to call.

2   Call at lunchtime.

3   Use the 'I'm worried' approach.

4   Ask if 'something's wrong'.

5   Call before or after normal business hours.

6   Use the 'I'm worried' approach and call senior executives.

Let's have a look at each of these.

Ask a colleague to call

Use this strategy so the person who generally answers the phone doesn't recognise your voice. Your colleague needs to sound really confident, with an upbeat, bright and breezy voice, and say something like:

'Oh, hi there. It's Amanda here. Just put me through to John please...'

The trick is to pretend she knows John really well.

Ask a colleague to call

As soon as your colleague has been transferred to your customer, they can pass the phone to you to take over the call. Your customer won't know there has been a 'switch'.

Call at lunchtime

The relief receptionist probably won't recognise your voice, and might put you straight through instead of screening your call.

'I'm worried'

You can also use the 'I'm worried' approach with the gatekeeper. The gatekeeper could be the receptionist or someone else. You can share your story:

'I'm a bit worried. Jack promised a cheque would arrive this week, but it hasn't. I've called four times to speak to him today, and I haven't been able to get hold of him at all.'

Ask if 'something's wrong'

Asking if 'something's wrong' is a show stopper. No-one likes any-one to think there's something wrong in their organisation – either if they own it or just work there.

You could say:

'I keep leaving messages for Kate in accounts, but she doesn't call me back. Is something wrong?'

Every time I've asked, *'Is something wrong?'*, people have gone to great lengths to pay their account pretty fast, just to confirm that nothing's wrong! It's a great way to get through to the right person and get paid.

Call before or after normal business hours

Another way to get through to an elusive person can be to call before or after hours. There will probably be no-one on reception, and you might get straight through to the person you're trying to reach.

Tell senior executives why you're 'worried'

Find out the names of different senior people in the company, and call them and tell them you're worried:

> 'I'm sorry to bother you [name], but I'm worried. Nancy promised us a large payment last Friday and it's Wednesday now. We haven't received it and I can't get hold of Nancy at all. I'm really worried something might be wrong. What do you think I should do?' (Pause and wait)

KEY POINTS

- Sometimes people are just busy. They have their own priorities. Getting your invoices paid is your priority, so you need to find a way to speak to the person who can pay your invoice.

- Sometimes people really are trying to avoid taking your call if they know they have overdue invoices, so you need to make a plan for how to get hold of them.

TO DO

1   Make a list of the customers you currently have where you are struggling to get past the gatekeeper and speak to the right person.

2   Try each of these strategies in turn until you get to speak to them.

30. CUSTOMER NOT PAYING BECAUSE OF A QUERY? HOW TO SOLVE IT INSTANTLY AND GET PAID

'One of the marks of successful people is they are action oriented.'

Brian Tracy, American/Canadian motivational speaker

Have you ever had a large invoice held for payment because of a small problem? I have, and because queries on invoices are valid reasons for non-payment, I've used this quick, brilliant strategy to fix the problem instantly and put my customer in a position to be able to pay.

It's called 'Oh, don't worry, I'll hold on', and this is how it works. Let's say that your customer says they need to get an approval from someone else in their company before they can pay your invoice. You say:

'Oh, don't worry, I'll just hold on here while you call him. That's absolutely fine.'

Or you can ask them to hold on. Let's say your customer says they need a proof of delivery from you to confirm the goods were delivered to them and signed for by one of their staff. You say:

> 'Mary, just hold on for me for half a minute while I call the warehouse and ask them to confirm.'

And if your customer needs a copy of your invoice or another document, you can say:

> 'I can email that to you right now. Just hold on for a second and I'll do it, then it's done, and we can get this all sorted right now.'

Using this positive, helpful type of dialogue does three things:

- It spurs your customer into action.

- It lets you keep control of the situation.

- It allows you to solve any problems during that call. That way you can avoid having to follow up later, which could delay your payment.

Even if you can't resolve the problem while you're on the phone, make a time to call back as soon as possible with the resolution. That's a customer service superhero approach, and you continue to keep control.

KEY POINT

Problems that are holding up payment of an invoice can often be solved very quickly over the phone and then your customer *can* pay.

TO DO

1   Which of your customers is holding on to the largest amount of money because they are waiting for a query to be resolved before they can pay the invoice?

2   How can you call them and use the 'oh, don't worry, I'll hold on' approach to resolve the situation and then ask them to pay? What's the shortest timeframe for that to happen?

31. HOW TO IMPROVE THE PAYMENT CYCLE OF LATE-PAYING CUSTOMERS

'Things do not change, we do.'

Henry Thoreau, American philosopher and historian

I had a customer who purchased around $2500 worth of services every week from us on 7-day terms. We always sent the invoices out on Friday and expected the customer to pay by the following Friday.

The trouble was that this customer's payment cycle was set up to pay suppliers monthly. By the time they paid us $2500 for the first week, we'd already sent out four more weekly invoices, so they owed us around $12,500. It looked like this:

	Week 1	Week 2	Week 3	Week 4	Week 5
Invoice	2500	2500	2500	2500	2500
Total owed	2500	5000	7500	10,000	12,500

As a small business, I couldn't let customers pay like that for weekly invoices. I needed that cash each week to pay my staff and my bills. I would have had to borrow money, and I couldn't afford to do that. I had to find a way to get this customer to pay on time.

We knew that the customer wasn't short of money, it was just that most of their suppliers were on 30-day terms and they'd set up their payment schedule accordingly. We just had to persuade them to go out of their way to pay us weekly.

So we decided to try to get to know our contact there better, and to get him to like us so he wouldn't mind making a special weekly payment for us.

The next Friday, we had four more invoices ready to send to him, but before we did we called him, and this is what we said:

'Hi Frank, I'm just about to email you the latest invoice. And there's one or two old items on your account I'd like to run through with you.'

And then I used an open question:

'When is a good time?'

I paused after asking 'When is a good time?', so that he filled in the gap and told me a good time.

Then, in a friendly way, I explained to Frank that we were a small business and that these invoices were on 7-day terms, and we couldn't afford to wait four or five weeks to be paid for each one. And then I asked:

'I know you pay all invoices to 30-day terms, but what can you do in special cases like ours? What is it that we both need to do so you can pay our invoices each week?'

Just by asking nicely and using 'what is it that we both need to do', Frank realised that he could make an exception and pay our invoices manually each week. And thereafter, we called him every Friday to let him know we were sending over the invoice and he paid us by the following Friday.

There's a lot to be said for simply asking.

'Ask until you get what you want.'

*Anthony Robbins, author, entrepreneur,
philanthropist and life coach*

KEY POINT

There is often a way that you can get existing customers to pay your invoices earlier, outside of their normal payment cycle. It might simply be a case of explaining your situation and then just asking.

TO DO

1   Pick three existing customers that you would like to pay earlier.

2   What do you need to change or put in place to start encouraging them to pay earlier?

3   Find out if your customer is paying late simply because they are paying to their payment cycle, not to your terms. Call them and explain your situation. Then ask them an 'open' question like, '**What** is it that we need to do so that you can make an exception and pay our invoices earlier?' (*then pause and wait for their answer*).

---

32. TWO WAYS TO SPEED UP A CUSTOMER'S PAYMENT PROCESS

'There's always a way – if you are committed.'

Anthony Robbins, author, entrepreneur,
philanthropist and life coach

THE 'LET ME DO IT FOR YOU' APPROACH

When I had my small business, there was no-one more interested in getting our invoices paid on time than me.

After the first few months, it wasn't me who called customers regarding payment of bills, but I did meet with our administrator once a week to find out how many overdue invoices we had, which customers hadn't paid, and what the reason was for non-payment.

Although we were a small company, a lot of our customers were quite big organisations, and after we'd been going about five years one of our big customers acquired another company. The new company had an excellent sales history and good customer base, however, it hadn't been very good at chasing payment of invoices. There were a lot of invoices very overdue for payment.

My business was a recruitment company specialising in collections and credit control staff, and we had been asked if we could supply experienced people to work with our customer for a few weeks to chase payment of all the old invoices in the newly acquired company. We soon found three experienced collections staff happy to work with our client and they all started work the following Monday.

Although they worked on our client's site, my company was their employer, and as such we were responsible for paying their salary each week and managing taxes and superannuation, as we did for all our employees. Four weeks went by, so we had already paid our three staff members four times, so we had 12 invoices outstanding with this customer that totalled almost $12,000.

When we called to speak to our customer, he was so busy that, naturally, he hadn't had time to even think about our invoices. That wasn't his priority. His priority was collecting all his company's overdue invoices.

> **Your customer's priority: getting their invoices paid.**
> **Your priority: getting your invoices paid.**

Getting *our* invoices paid was our priority, so what we did to help our customer achieve his priorities, while we achieved ours, was to use the 'let me do it for you' approach.

We learnt from our customer that there were four steps to getting invoices paid in his organisation:

1   Log them with the accounts payable department.

2   The accounts payable department sent them back to our contact for signature.

3   Our contact signed them and sent them back to accounts payable.

4   Accounts payable made the payment to us.

We suggested to our customer that, as he was so busy, he should let us organise the signing off system with accounts payable: 'Let us do all that for you'.

We called our contact in accounts payable, explained the situation to her, and asked for her help. It's amazing what happens when you ask for help. Most people want to be helpful, and she was no exception. We explained that our contact was so busy, he hadn't had time to even think about our invoices, but he was happy with our service and was happy to authorise our invoices for payment.

Then we asked, if we emailed copies of all 12 invoices to her, would she please print them out, log them on her system, and then take them around to our contact this afternoon and wait while he signed them off for payment? She agreed.

We called our contact back, told him that Alice would bring the invoices to him that afternoon, and wait while he signed them. He was so happy that we had taken away a task for him that he was ready and waiting for Alice that afternoon.

We then called Alice again. She was pleased to have been able to help us and the Line Manager. We explained that the invoices were overdue, and as a small company that money was quite important to us. Would she be able to do a special payment for us that afternoon?

By this time we had built a relationship with Alice and we'd been working together on a problem which between us we'd solved. She was happy to oblige, and we got our payment the following day.

Our staff members stayed with that client for another four months. Every Monday morning, we called Alice: 'We've got our invoices here, Alice. If we email them to you, will you please take them around to the Line Manager to sign off?'

The answer was always yes. We'd built our relationship, and Alice was ready to help us every step of the way. We had become a 'team'. We were all in this together solving a potential problem. Every week, she paid us straight away.

Asking customers to 'let us do that for you' turned out to be a great way to get our invoices paid on time. Customers are always busy, and let's face it, generally paying suppliers' invoices isn't going to be a priority. Offering to do something that makes your customers' lives easier is a great way to build relationships with people. They get to like you because you're so helpful, and you keep control of the process and get invoices paid at the same time.

It might sound as if we were spending time doing someone else's job, but we got our money in faster, built strong relationships, customers liked us and our customer service attitude, and gave us more business. It worked really well, and the benefits were huge. We used 'let me do it for you' often.

To keep control while you resolve an issue you can adapt one of the following phrases, which have all worked well for me in the past:

- **'Let me do that for you,** Sarah, and I'll get back to you straight away. Will you be in your office at twelve o'clock today?'

- **'Let me see if I can resolve this for you this morning,** Michael. Will you be there after lunch, about two o'clock?'

- **'Can't find our invoice? Would copies help?** Let me send you some now for you to check over, and then I'll call you back this afternoon to make sure everything is okay. Are you there around 3 pm this afternoon? Good, I'll call you back.'

These examples are marvellous, service-oriented offers to resolve a query. If you use the word 'you' and the person's name, it will also make the person feel really important and valued.

HOW I GOT CUSTOMERS TO PAY *BEFORE* THE INVOICE WAS DUE FOR PAYMENT

'Our attitude towards others determines
their attitude towards us.'

Earl Nightingale, motivational speaker and author

Many years ago, when I started to work as a collections officer for a large multinational corporation, I quickly realised that the more helpful I was to customers, and the more I developed a friendly but professional relationship, the more helpful they were to me.

When I went out of my way to resolve queries and issues quickly for customers, they would go out of their way to make sure we got paid on time.

One year, as it got towards our company's financial year end, everyone in the department I worked in had collections targets to achieve. We each had to collect a certain amount of money from customers to make sure the company had as much money in the bank as possible at the close of the year.

I was working towards being the best collector in our department, and I suddenly realised that maybe, if I called some of my biggest customers, the ones that usually paid at the beginning of the month, maybe they would pay a few days earlier than normal.

I called them one by one and asked them to pay one or two days earlier than normal, just so I could reach my collections target … and guess what?

They did. They paid early.

Just remembering it now makes me glow. It's such a positive illustration of how you can build a strong working relationship with people and they will then go out of their way to help you if you ask.

KEY POINTS

- Doing something that makes customers' lives easier is a great way to get people to like you and build strong relationships with them.

- When you build a strong, friendly business relationship with customers and go out of your way to help them, they will almost certainly return the compliment and go out of their way to help you.

TO DO

1 Which top three customers would you like to have a better working relationship with?

2 Decide on three things you can do to start to improve your relationship with them.

33. HOW TO USE EMAIL TO HELP YOU GET PAID

'I would have written a shorter letter, but I did not have the time.'

Blaise Pascal, The Provincial Letters: Letter XVI (4 December 1656 – translated), French mathematician and theologian

Email can really help you get paid on time in a few different ways. We've already talked about using email to send invoices the fast way – but email can also help you get paid fast too.

It can be especially helpful for writing a brief note to confirm an agreement that's been made with your customer. For example, confirming a promise to pay after you have sorted out a query and raised a credit note is a really good reason to email.

Sending an email setting out the situation after the credit has been raised can make the situation very clear for your customer so they know what to do next (see following illustration).

Whenever you write an email, always address it to the right person. If your email is important, call to let the person know that you will be sending it and ask them to look out for it. Or call after sending the email to make sure it has been received and that it addresses all of the current issues.

HOW TO GET PAID WITH EMAIL

GOOD EMAILS =

✓ Short and precise
✓ Use bullet points for clarity
✓ Confirm promises and
  agreements

Here are some examples of emails we used in my business to get our customers' undivided attention. Let's take the example of attaching a credit note.

Subject: Three May invoices – total $11,839.50 + Credit No T54 $867.00 (attached)

Hi Charles,

Re: Your O/No AH2367.

As promised, please find attached the three May invoices together with our credit note T54 to adjust the price on all three.

10 May Invoice 5635	$2,000.00
23 May Invoice 5865	$4,500.00
28 May Invoice 5935	$5,339.50
	$11,839.50
30 June Credit T54	($867.00)
Total now due	**$10,972.50**

As discussed, I believe this resolves your query, but I will call you shortly just to confirm.

Best regards,

Jan

Subject: Invoice #94567 dated 12.09.18 total $1,457.30 (attached)

Hi James,

Just a note to confirm our conversation today re the five green widgets missing from the shipment detailed on the above invoice.

As you know, while you were on the line, I arranged for our warehouse to overnight courier the missing five to you tonight, marked for your attention.

As discussed, this invoice is now overdue for payment and, as soon as the widgets are received, you have very kindly offered to include this invoice in your payment run on Friday.

I will call you after lunch tomorrow to confirm safe receipt as promised.

Thanks so much for your help in resolving this matter quickly; it's much appreciated.

Best regards,

Jan

End the email with a brief note to let your customer know you will call tomorrow to confirm they have received the email and that they don't have any further queries.

Calling your customer gives you the opportunity to gently remind them of the date the invoice is due for payment. It also gives you a chance to continue to build the relationship.

KEY POINTS

- It's been proven that people don't always read large blocks of text, and they often don't read down to the bottom of an email. They just 'skim', so make your emails clear and precise.

- Use email to confirm what's already been agreed by phone.

- Re-read your email before you send it. Try to delete some text to make it shorter while still being clear about all the facts the customer needs.

TO DO

1 Which customer do you have that might be a little confused about what they owe?

2 Write a brief, succinct email to clarify the amounts for them.

3 Call them to let them know you are sending an email to 'clarify' the account. Call again afterwards to confirm receipt of your email and see if there's anything else they need from you to be able to pay the invoices on time.

RED FLAGS! HOW TO SPOT ONE AND WHAT TO DO ABOUT IT

A red flag is widely recognised as a danger sign and is often used in business in the context of a customer *never* paying an account (for any reason). The amount on the invoice is at risk of becoming a bad debt.

In a situation where a customer is *never* going to pay or *never going to be able to pay* an invoice or invoices, then it becomes a bad debt and you have not only lost your money as the face value of the invoice but a great deal more.

This part of the book explains the real cost of bad debt (which is *huge*), why a business owner must do all they can to avoid having a bad debt, and what to do if you think a bad debt might be imminent.

34. THE REAL COST OF A BAD DEBT

If a customer goes out of business owing you money, or they absolutely refuse to pay for some reason, then you will have a bad debt. Bad debts are crippling and will cost you much more money than just the value on the invoices – and losing money is the last thing we can afford to do as small business owners.

Here's an example of how to work out what a bad debt *really* costs you.

- Bad debt amount $1000.

- Profit margin 5% (for every $100 of sales you make a profit of $5).

Amount of new business required to cover the $1000 debt is $20,000.

Profit is hard to come by. In a small business, if you don't get paid, that bad debt can make a massive dent in your profits. Too many bad debts and lack of profits and your business will not survive. It will have to close.

> The longer an invoice is outstanding, the more likely it is that it will never be paid.

HOW TO REDUCE THE CHANCE OF A BAD DEBT

One way to reduce the chance of a bad debt is to make sure your customers have a good track record of paying their existing suppliers. Here's how we 'credit checked' new customers:

- Before we accepted an order, if we didn't know or hadn't heard of the business we made sure our potential new customer was a valid company.

    (You can do that in many ways – by researching through Google and looking through their website for information and researching whether the business has officially registered with local, state or federal authorities. You can check to see if they belong to any industry-specific organisations, or you can use a company credit report to check the legitimacy of a company and their financial performance. Or, you can outsource all that research to an external organisation. Equifax or Dun & Bradstreet (now Illion) are pretty much household names, but there are a host of smaller local credit scoring companies to choose from.)

- The way we did it in my business was to ask new customers to give us the names and contact details of five of their existing suppliers. We'd ring those companies to find out if our potential new customer paid their bills on time. We did that before we did any work and before we set up an account for a new customer.

- If the feedback was that our potential new customer always paid late or argued about the bill, we'd have to make a decision. If for some reason we wanted to trade with the customer regardless, we asked for payment before we started work on an order.

In the next chapter we'll look at how to spot a 'red flag' and what action to take to make sure you don't lose your money.

KEY POINTS

- The longer an invoice is outstanding, the more likely it is it will never be paid.

- To recover your financial position after losing money as a bad debt, you will have to sell (and be paid for) much much more than the value of the bad debt.

- Not all business is good business. Choose your customers carefully.

TO DO

If you don't already, decide now how you will credit check all new customers before accepting the first order.

35. HOW TO SPOT RED FLAGS AND WHAT TO DO ABOUT THEM

'As with almost any problem, the best way to
stop debt collection problems is before they start.
The second-best solution is to identify a problem early.'

Dean Kaplan, Director, The Kaplan Group

RED FLAGS

A 'red flag' is a concern that there may be something wrong in a customer's business and so your money could be at risk. 'Red flag' is a term used generally when you get the feeling or an 'inkling' that the customer either cannot or will not pay their account.

Red flags can be:

- A change in your customer's tone of voice that makes you feel uneasy.

- A payment is overdue, and you've been unable to get a commitment to pay from your customer.

- When your contact hesitates answering your questions.

- Decision makers could be hard to get hold of (for example, they're 'travelling' or 'they're sick').

- Changes in your customer's payments with no explanation; for example, making part payments, or late payment with no explanation.

- Intuitively you feel that the customer either cannot or will not pay their account.

- Negative rumours about the customer or something adverse in the press.

When you come across this type of situation, you need to act fast because your customer could be in financial difficulty. It's your money that's at risk and that money is very important to you, so you need to find out quickly what the real situation is.

Your customer has received the goods or service. You've kept your part of the bargain. You need your money back, so don't delay – act *now*.

Contact your customer as soon as you become concerned. Use open questions and be gentle but persistent until you find out what the real problem is and when you'll receive your money. Have all your notes of previous conversations with the customer in front of you before you speak to the customer. Remember, knowledge is power.

I've previously used these approaches to uncover what's wrong:

- The 'I'm worried' approach (chapter 29).

- The 'Is something wrong?' approach (chapter 29).

KEY POINTS

- The longer an invoice is outstanding, the more likely it will never be paid.

- When you get the feeling or an 'inkling' that the customer either cannot or will not pay their account – that's a 'red flag'. Your money may be at risk.

- You need to act fast and find out quickly what the real situation is.

- Be persistent until you find out what the real problem is.

TO DO

1   Make a list of current potential 'red flag' customers.

2   Ask yourself a series of questions to determine if it's a potential bad debt:

   - How long have we known and traded with this customer?

   - What is the customer's payment history?

   - Do we have references from other companies that this customer is trading with?

   - Can we call the referees and ask if they are also not being paid?

3   Decide what action to take:

   - Use the 'I'm worried' and/or the 'is something wrong' approaches.

   - Can you visit the customer to find out the situation? If it's a large amount, definitely do that if it's possible and realistic.

36. COMPANY WITH STRANGE PAYMENT POLICIES? RED FLAG!

Here's some payment behaviour that you need to watch out for. These could also be a sign that you need to keep a close eye on this customer:

- Some companies only pay when someone calls and asks for payment.

- Some companies pay those people who 'shout the loudest', the ones that call the most often, or they'll only pay when the supplier calls for the sixth time.

Regular payment delays could be a sign to reconsider trading with a customer. What you'll allow your customers to get away with depends on your business policies, but here's a couple of things to consider:

- The longer an invoice is outstanding, the more likely it is that it will never be paid at all. It will become a bad debt.

- The longer the invoice is outstanding, the less profit will be made.

If you have a seriously overdue account:

- keep calm but keep the pressure up

- call often – at least every day until payment is made

- call before or after standard business hours (owners often arrive at work early or stay late).

If you choose your customers wisely, and follow the five steps in this book, you shouldn't have to deal with many such situations, but it's a good idea to be prepared and have fast, easy access to a professional collections company in case you ever need expert help.

If you really feel there's something wrong, and your relationship with the customer has broken down, realise your money is potentially at risk. Don't delay further – pass it to an expert quickly.

If the company is in financial difficulty, the longer you delay, the more chance you will never be paid.

If there's a time when you think you can see a big red flag waving very strongly in a stiff breeze, take some fast action to safeguard your money.

KEY POINTS

- The longer an invoice is outstanding, the more likely it is that it will never be paid at all. It will become a bad debt.

- The longer an invoice is outstanding, the less profit you'll make.

TO DO

1   If you currently have some seriously overdue accounts, decide what action you'll take to recover your money.

2   If you don't already have access to a collection agency, ask other business owners for recommendations so you can contact an expert quickly if you ever need one.

37. EXISTING CUSTOMER SUDDENLY PAYING SLOWLY? RED FLAG!

'You can't manage what you don't measure.'

Peter F. Drucker, American management consultant, educator and author

As a small business owner, you can never 'rest on your laurels' for long. If you want to have a successful and profitable business, you need to be vigilant and continually measure two important aspects of the business: sales and getting paid for sales.

Sometimes your oldest customers get into difficulty. Long-established businesses can fail. A change of ownership or management might mean customers move business elsewhere. Sales plummet, and your customer might go into liquidation – and your outstanding invoices might become a bad debt. In some cases, a customer's financial demise, where they cannot pay their suppliers' bills, can send their supplier into liquidation or bankruptcy. Don't let that be you.

> A sale is only a sale when it's paid for.

Because I needed to pay staff weekly, I needed cash flowing into my company constantly, so I learnt to monitor both sales and accounts receivable (debtors) every week. I was aware too that as invoices remained unpaid for longer and longer, the more chance they have of not being paid at all. If an invoice was overdue I always wanted to understand why the customer hadn't paid.

If I heard of changes in the way a customer was placing orders or paying invoices, I was aware that could be a 'red flag'. These are some of the excuses I've heard when a customer hasn't been able to pay their invoice on time:

- The business has been sold to another company and they've been told to hold all payments during the takeover.

- The customer is waiting for their debtors to pay.

- They are waiting for a new cheque book or the cheque's in the mail. (These don't work well now most payments are electronic.)

- They're just building a new warehouse.

- They've just moved.

- The accounts payable person has left.

- The boss is sick.

- The boss is on holiday.

If a business is in a position where they don't have enough money to pay their bills, it's highly unlikely they will tell you. Most likely, they will be working hard to try to keep creditors at bay.

Whenever I noticed customers paying their account differently to normal, I monitored the situation – I put it on my high-awareness list and stepped up the information-gathering process. If the debt became a loss, I knew how much more we'd have to sell to make up the lost profit.

There's no need to panic at this stage because there could be a legitimate reason why payments have slowed. If you credit check your customers and get to know them and their business, so you only supply genuine businesses, they should pay in the end (but not always, so be aware). Your customer might just have an acute cashflow shortage, but whatever the problem is, *you need to know* so you can take the appropriate action.

SUPPLYING CUSTOMERS WHO ALREADY HAVE OVERDUE INVOICES

If your customer is a big company and another department in that business places a new order, and you already have an invoice that they haven't paid, take the order and then call them a few minutes later and gently say that the order is ready to be made up but there's a problem with the account. It's overdue and needs to be paid before sending any more goods or providing any more services. If you dispatch more goods or provide more services, and the customer can't pay, it would be cheaper for you to open the window and throw your hard-earned cash out.

KEY POINTS

- You can only manage things that you can measure. Keep a check on your debtors as much as your sales.

- Remember, it's *your* money and you're entitled to it.

- If you collect payment of your invoices when they are due, if your customer does fail, you'll avoid losing several months' invoices. Don't let their demise be yours as well.

TO DO

1   Before sending a new order, check to see if the customer has paid all previous bills promptly and doesn't have any invoices overdue.

2   Check your accounts receivable (debtors) list at least once a week. See who hasn't paid and follow up promptly.

3   Be aware that changes in payment patterns – or changes in placing orders – can be a red flag, even with large companies.

38. NEW CUSTOMER PAYING SLOWLY? RED FLAG!

You can educate new customers to pay your invoices on time right from the very first order they place with you (see chapter 6, 'How to train new customers to pay on time'). However, occasionally I've had new customers who behaved like naughty children. They haven't paid by the due date and seemed to want to try their luck at holding on to their money – *my* money! I've had an instance where a customer has said to me, 'We never pay our bills on time.'

Like a naughty child, he was just trying his luck. If I had let him get away with paying late he would have kept doing it, so I tried to charm him and make him smile by giving a light-hearted response: 'Gosh, you're lucky to get away with that. All our customers pay us on time. I'm sure we can come to an agreement that suits us both.'

If saying something like that to one of your customers (who you have supplied but they haven't paid!) doesn't seem the right thing to say, and you aren't sure what to do, just consider a few things:

- When someone places an order with your company, unless otherwise agreed, they are agreeing to pay within your trading terms (not theirs).

- The longer an invoice is not paid, the more likely it is never to be paid (and it will become a bad debt – you'll lose your money and it will cost you much more than the invoice value).

- Think about how valuable this customer really is to you – and think about your bank balance. What profit are you making from them?

'If the customer will not [pay on time], it can be to your advantage to introduce them to your best competitor. After all, if they cause a loss for your business, they will almost certainly cause a loss to your competitor.'

Kim Radok, owner of Credit Matters Pty Ltd

Or if you feel that they might be a valuable customer in the future, it might be worth visiting with them (see chapter 40). Meeting a customer face to face at their place of work is a brilliant relationship-building exercise. Almost every time I've met a customer face to face, the relationship has improved enormously.

KEY POINTS

- New customers might 'try their luck' at paying late. They are trying to use you as a bank. Don't let them.

- If you aren't making a profit from a customer, let them go to a competitor.

- When someone places an order with your company, unless already agreed differently, they are agreeing to pay within your trading terms (not theirs).

- The longer an invoice is not paid, the more likely it is never to be paid at all.

TO DO

1   Visit any large new customers as a priority. Start to build your business relationship and get them 'on your side' straight away so they pay you fast.

2   Check which customers pay you late and work out if you are making a profit from the transactions (after all, you're in business to make a profit). If you aren't, decide if it is worth keeping them as a customer.

39. WHAT TO SAY IF YOUR PROMISED PAYMENT DOESN'T TURN UP

If your customer promises a payment, ask them which method they are using to send it to you, then make a diary note to check and see if it turns up as promised.

If it doesn't turn up a day or so after you think it should, and you have a suspicion that this is a delaying tactic on the customer's part, you need something powerful to spur the customer into action – and this is it. It makes me smile when I think about using these tactics. They appear gentle and caring, but in fact they 'hit the customer right between the eyes' and galvanise them into action to get your payment to you immediately.

What you do is start telling people in that organisation that you are 'really worried' about something relating to the payment, and then you ask, 'Is something wrong?' (This is a combination of two strategies we've looked at earlier.) Keep a light, positive and caring tone to your voice. You want people to like you and want to talk to you – aggression and bad temper don't get a good result.

Here's an example of how I've asked a receptionist 'if something is wrong':

'I'm sorry to bother you but I'm really worried. Nancy promised us a large payment on Friday and it's Wednesday now. We haven't received it and I can't get hold of Nancy at all. I'm really worried something might be wrong. What do you think I should do?'

The moment people hear that someone is 'really worried', they start worrying too. The receptionist went to Nancy in a worried state.

People don't like to think that anyone is worried about something relating to them, their employer or their business, and they will go out of their way to make sure that person is worried no more. I always got my payment.

I've said very similar things to owners of businesses too. Owners hate the thought that there could be something in their business that someone is worried about or that employees or suppliers might think 'there's something wrong'.

'I'm really worried' and 'is something wrong' are gentle but powerful strategies that always get great results. You can use either (or both together, like I have here) in instances where you've been promised a payment that doesn't arrive.

A TOP QUESTION TO ASK!

Here are some more examples of when I've used it to get a result:

Talking to an accounts payable department in a big company:

'Jack in your warehouse said he would sign that invoice off, get it back to you and ask you to pay it last Thursday, but you still don't have it?

Oh dear. I've tried calling to speak to Jack for the last three days but no-one answers the phone. I'm really worried. What do you think I should do?' (Pause to allow the person to answer after asking this open question.)

Talking to a Line Manager:

'Hi Helen, last Thursday Susan promised she would sort out those four old invoices with you and get back to me.

She seemed very keen to help but I haven't heard anything from her since then and can't get hold of her. I'm really worried – what do you think I should do?' (Pause to allow the person to answer after asking this open question.)

Talking to the owner (owners are proud of their company and would never want others to think there might be 'something wrong' with either their business or anyone working in their business):

'Hello Mr Smith, I'm so sorry to bother you with this but I've recently been chatting with Sandra in your accounts department and she promised to send a payment last Wednesday.

I've kept my eyes open for it but it's now Tuesday and it still hasn't arrived, and I can't get hold of her at all. No-one seems to know where she is. I'm really worried. Is something wrong?'(Pause to allow the person to answer after asking this open question.)

KEY POINTS

- When a customer promises a payment, always make a diary note and follow up to see if it arrives as promised.

- No-one likes anyone to think that there could be something to worry about in their company – regardless of their position in it.

- If you say 'I'm really worried', make sure you sound worried, and caring.

TO DO

Which three customers are you really worried about because they haven't paid? Try this tactic on each of them.

40. BIG MONEY AT STAKE? CUSTOMER WANTS A DISCOUNT? GO VISITING!

Meeting your customer can make a big difference to when they pay your invoices. You might have heard the expression, 'When people like you they buy from you.' Well, that's true. It's not often we buy from people we don't like.

It's also true about getting invoices paid. If your customer likes you, they are much more likely to pay you before they pay someone they don't like. Building a positive business relationship with your customer so they get to like you will help you get paid sooner.

> When people like you they buy from you.
>
> When people like you they pay you too.

You can get to know customers over the phone but meeting a customer face to face takes relationship building to a whole new level.

It's not always possible to meet a customer, but if it is possible, it is really worth doing, especially if you have some large-value accounts or potential large-value accounts.

Here's why…

WILL THIS BE A 'GOOD CUSTOMER' FOR ME? YOU HAVE TO DECIDE FOR YOURSELF

When I had my business, the fourth-largest telecoms company in the country asked to place several orders with us. They had a large team and doing business with them could have amounted to tens of thousands of dollars. They were considered to be a progressive and successful company, which was just the sort of customer we wanted, so I went to meet with them.

When I went to their office, it was just as I had read: everyone seemed high energy and progressive – but somehow, I just didn't feel comfortable. I had heard 'on the grapevine' that they were slow to pay their bills and sitting in their office I had the feeling things weren't quite as they appeared.

Because of the feelings I had at the meeting I declined to work with them – although in the end, that was a relatively easy decision because they wanted heavily discounted rates. Companies that want discounted rates always send up a 'reg flag' with me. My feeling was that we charged a fair price for a fair transaction. If we discounted, we would be saying that we were overcharging, which we weren't. My policy was not to discount.

Less than a year later that company collapsed into administration. My hunch had been right. Had we worked with them, firstly we would have had to discount, and secondly, when they collapsed, they would have owed us money which we wouldn't have been able to recoup, and that would have been a substantial bad debt for us.

Going to visit customers can help in three ways:

- You get a 'vibe' of both the customer and their business (vibes are valuable – see chapter 41, 'Trust your intuition').

- It can help you decide that this is or isn't the type of business you want and if trading with them will be profitable for you.

- You can start to build or grow a relationship – so the customer gets to like you and so pays you on time.

THREE EASY WAYS TO GET TO MEET YOUR CUSTOMER

It's easier to build strong relationships with people face to face, but all customers are busy. If I asked a customer for a meeting it would sound as if it would take up a lot of time. So, I made it sound like it would be a super-quick visit and I'd just be there for a few minutes. I'd say:

'I'm just passing by your office on Friday. Would it put you out if I drop in to introduce myself?'

"I'LL JUST DROP IN TO SAY HI!..."

Or:

'I'm in the same building next Tuesday. Is it okay with you if I stick my head in the door to say hi?'

"I'LL JUST STICK MY HEAD IN TO SAY HI!..."

Or:

> *'I'm out with our salesman next Wednesday when he's coming in to see you. I could drop that paperwork off to you then if that suits you?'*

Using 'dropping in' and 'passing by' and 'putting my head in the door' turned out to be really easy ways to meet customers. No-one minds someone 'dropping in' for a couple of minutes. I found that when I did meet them, as soon as the ice was broken and we started chatting, I was usually offered coffee or tea and was encouraged to stay with them longer than a couple of minutes.

The next time I spoke to them, the conversation was so much easier. They were keen to be helpful, and that included making sure we got paid on time.

The only time I would ask for a 'meeting' was if the account was in a mess or needed a thorough reconciliation – that's better done with both parties together and can take some time, so it needs organising in advance.

If it's at all possible, visiting a customer is an excellent way to develop a strong, mutually beneficial business relationship.

KEY POINTS

- Relationships can be built more easily face to face. The stronger your relationship is with your customer the more likely they are to pay you on time.

- If a customer is buying substantial amounts from you – for example, 10% of your monthly invoicing – that could be a big risk for you and it's worthwhile getting to know them.

- When people like you they buy from you.

- When people like you they pay you too.

TO DO

1   Decide which of your large customers you should know better and have a closer relationship with. It's *your money* at risk.

2   Make a date and time to 'drop in for a moment to say hi'.

41. TRUST YOUR INTUITION

'It is through science that we prove,
but through intuition that we discover.'

Henri Poincare, French mathematician and philosopher

Having been a successful small business owner, I can see the value in systems, strategies, data, and having 'checks and balances'. There's also something valuable that's inbuilt in us all. It's very powerful: your *intuition*.

> Intuition: 'the ability to understand something instinctively, without the need for conscious reasoning'.

Intuition can be powerful, but I would never suggest people act solely on their intuition. I've employed people just using my intuition and have made several mistakes! Intuition can act as a reminder to check the facts before you make a decision.

Early humans used intuition a lot – there were lots of dangers around them and they didn't have too much else to go by. As we've gone through the centuries, we humans have lost some of our ability to develop and act on our intuition because there are now more facts available to check, but intuition is still a powerful force and should not be ignored. Around collecting money, it works well to listen to your intuition.

Without money continually flowing into your business, your business can fail. Listening to your intuition and taking swift action can save you money (see how it saved me from working with a telecoms company that soon went bust in chapter 40). It may even be the difference between the success and failure of your business.

These are some of the things to look out for that might ring 'alarm' bells:

- A customer being very hard to get hold of.

- A customer paying later than usual, especially over more than one payment cycle.

- A new customer paying slowly.

- Customers making part payments.

- Unhappy people in your customer's business.

- A big turnover of staff.

- The customer making staff members redundant.

- A customer telling you they have 'cashflow problems' because their customers aren't paying on time. Now you have read this book, you might offer them some suggestions about how to get their own invoices paid faster (I've done that many times).

- Customers placing larger than normal orders when they haven't paid their account up to date (this can be an indication that they haven't paid another supplier and the supplier has refused them further credit).

- A change of senior management or ownership.

See also chapter 35 on 'red flags'.

If you get an 'uneasy feeling' that something is wrong when you are trying to get your invoice paid, that could be your intuition telling you that there could be a problem and that you need to take some action

You don't want to make a mistake by thinking there's a problem when there isn't, nor do you want to create a problem, but if you acknowledge your intuitive thoughts and then make some gentle enquires, if nothing is wrong you don't have egg on your face. But, if you gather a few more facts and realise that something might be wrong, it can save you adding to the debt by shipping more goods to the customer.

Following your intuition can also allow you to 'get to the front of the payment queue' and recover your money if there is a problem. I've done that many times. Forewarned is forearmed, and in the case of something so important as your money, you need to take action straight away.

KEY POINTS

- If you feel 'something isn't right', don't ignore it. It could be your intuition trying to warn you. Take the time to check a few facts.

- If everything *is* right, all it's cost you is just a little bit of your time.

- If something *isn't* right, you may have saved a fortune – even your business.

TO DO

1   List your customers who have seriously overdue invoices.

2   How do you *feel* about them not paying? Do you *feel* confident that your money is safe?

3   Make a list of what facts you need to check and take action – just in case something *isn't* right and your money might be at risk.

42. WHY AND HOW YOU SHOULD KEEP TRACK OF CASH AS MUCH AS YOU KEEP TRACK OF SALES

'You can only manage what you measure.'

Pastor Rick Warren, American author

Can you quickly lay your hands on what your company sold last week, or last month? I'm sure you can. Most business owners are very careful and diligent when it comes to keeping track of sales. If you ask them what they've sold this month or last week, they probably know. And of course, it's crucial to know how much you are selling; after all, if there are no sales there's no company.

Cash is equally as important. If there's no cash, there's no company, but business owners are often vague about how much money they're owed (invoiced and not yet paid) – 'we're owed heaps' – and what money is promised and when it is due to arrive – 'why don't customers just pay?'

The truth is, if there's no sales there's no future for a company and, if there's not enough cash coming in, there's no company either.

> ### Zero sales = No company
> ### Zero cashflow = No company

Sales figures and cashflow figures were pride of place in my small business.

As much as I kept my eye on sales, after potential non-payment of a huge amount in the first year, I never lost focus on who paid (or rather who hadn't paid) on time. I always wanted to know what the reason was, what next steps we needed to take to retrieve that money, and importantly, what I could put in place to stop that happening again.

Every sale can be a great win, but until it's been paid for it's a debt to you. Here's what it owes you:

- the hours you or your employees have spent providing your service to the customer (time is money)

  or

- the costs of the goods you bought – and have had to pay for – and the time your business has spent moving those goods on to your customer

  or

- both of the above.

If you have accounting software, there should be a facility to run a daily, weekly or monthly report. What you need is a list of all customers who owe you money, how much in total, and then broken down into how old and the value of each individual invoice.

Although we used accounting software, our package didn't do exactly what we wanted it to so we created this report ourselves using Excel (see page 202).

KEY POINT

Just as you keep a record of what has been sold today, this week and this month, it is equally as important to keep a daily track of what is owed and what has been received today.

I managed the day-to-day running of my business by checking those two reports – often daily, certainly weekly, and more formally monthly, along with all the other important figures.

TO DO

Decide on a collection target each week. Like most goals or targets, begin with the end in mind. If you sell on 30-day terms this could work well for you:

- Work out the total in dollars of the invoices that are due for payment this month.

- Split that dollar figure into four or five – that's your weekly target.

- Try to collect *more* than your target every week.

- Have a list of what amounts are owing for each client, and mark off amounts that are paid each day. (You can track all this as shown in the following example spreadsheet.)

Customer Name	1-7 Days Old	8-14 Days Old	15-21 Days Old	22-28 Days Old - Now Overdue	28 and over old - Now overdue	60 and over - seriously overdue	90 and over - seriously overdue	Customer Balance
Sarsons Entertainment	$1,905.20	$1,905.20	$1,905.20	$1,905.20	$3,810.40	$0.00	$0.00	$11,431.20
Entry Bankers	$20,590.83	$21,638.22	$19,639.77	$14,434.10	$29,743.67	$0.00	-$1,355.64	$104,690.95
Farmers Alliance	$1,746.13	$2,396.42	$0.00	$0.00	$15.97	$0.00	$0.00	$4,158.52
KYN Market Traders	$0.00	$2,083.61	$1,569.14	$0.00	$1,594.86	$0.00	$0.00	$5,247.61
Blue Stream International	$2,602.50	$2,644.82	$2,792.93	$2,792.93	$0.00	$0.00	$0.00	$10,833.18
Fortheringtons Cakes	$1,857.90	$0.00	$0.00	$0.00	$0.00	$0.00	$0.00	$1,857.90
Tremendous Medical Solutions	$1,773.34	$1,773.34	$1,773.34	$1,773.34	$1,384.06	$0.00	$0.00	$8,477.42
Braintree Liqor Merchants	$1,678.74	$1,678.74	$0.00	$0.00	$0.00	$0.00	$0.00	$3,357.48
Crisswells Pharmaceuticals	$9,126.76	$7,547.62	$0.00	$1,760.97	$0.00	$0.00	-$4,796.34	$13,639.01
Turner and Turner Industries	$1,608.34	$1,608.34	$0.00	$0.00	$0.00	$0.00	$0.00	$3,216.68
Foresight Security	$1,319.24	$1,395.85	$1,344.78	$1,395.85	$1,395.85	$0.00	-$8,067.40	-$1,215.83
Chambers Security	$1,960.62	$1,880.59	$773.58	$1,973.95	$1,973.95	$0.00	-$642.38	$7,920.31
Davos Systems Asia Pacific	$0.00	$0.00	$0.00	$0.00	$0.00	$0.00	-$998.34	-$998.34
Toppers Paper Merchants	$0.00	$2,000.63	$0.00	$0.00	$0.00	$0.00	$0.00	$2,000.63
Jenkins Cosmetic Suppliers	$3,270.07	$1,985.61	$3,290.08	$2,193.35	$10,712.96	$3,026.27	$0.00	$24,478.34
Bright and Breezy Bagels	$685.91	$0.00	$0.00	$0.00	$0.00	$0.00	$0.00	$685.91
Blue Access all Hours	$1,797.69	$1,797.69	$0.00	$0.00	$0.00	$0.00	$0.00	$3,595.38
Superfine Energy	$1,786.13	$1,786.13	$0.00	$0.00	$0.00	$0.00	$0.00	$3,572.26
Medway Group	$1,586.08	$1,607.52	$0.00	$0.00	$0.00	$0.00	$0.00	$3,193.60
Greater West Food Stores	$3,265.55	$3,197.04	$3,288.38	$0.00	$0.00	$0.00	$0.00	$9,750.97
Greater Western Steel Trading	$0.00	$9,122.03	$1,762.31	$1,417.00	$0.00	$0.00	$0.00	$12,301.34
Proctor Partridge Company	$10,185.45	$1,732.50	$1,316.70	$0.00	$0.00	$0.00	$0.00	$13,234.65
Ya Hum Group	$0.00	$1,306.47	$0.00	$0.00	$0.00	$0.00	$0.00	$1,306.47
Clear and Bright Environmental Services	$1,998.04	$1,998.04	$1,998.04	$0.00	$0.00	$0.00	$0.00	$5,994.12
Painters Corporation	$1,748.18	$1,748.18	$1,748.18	$0.00	$0.00	$0.00	$0.00	$5,244.54
Last Chance Finance	$0.00	$1,428.90	$0.00	$0.00	$0.00	$0.00	$0.00	$1,428.90
Total	**$72,492.70**	**$76,263.49**	**$43,202.43**	**$29,646.69**	**$50,631.72**	**$3,026.27**	**-$15,860.10**	**$259,403.20**
Actual	28%	29%	17%	11%	20%	1%	-6%	100%
Target	71%	10%	11%	6%	1%	1%	0%	0%

(average number of days it takes our clients to pay) Average DSO 24.34, Target 21.00

325	YTD Days
13.36	YTD Turnover
3,464,341	YTD Billing

How to Calculate:
Use any period eg a month
Divide total amount outstanding by total sales and multiply by 30

HOW TO MAKE GETTING PAID GREAT FUN

'We find no real satisfaction or happiness in life
without obstacles to conquer and goals to achieve.'

Maxwell Maltz, author of Psycho-Cybernetics;
ideas to improve self-image

If you can't imagine how collecting payments can be fun, let me explain how I've made it into a fun task many times and with many people.

A few years before I stared my own small business, I took a new job with a company that had completely neglected their debtors for months and months.

It had been a private company and had been bought 12 months ago by a large international corporation. Since the takeover, the focus had been entirely on sales and building a new sales team. Collecting outstanding accounts had been completely neglected.

It was a medium-sized company, and the amount that customers owed was huge – over £4 million. Almost 50% of the £4 million was four months old or more. It was a massive challenge.

Due to the upheaval, three staff members had left the accounts receivable department. There was just one staff member left who was trying to manage all the invoices. She was completely overwhelmed and depressed. No-one had contacted any customers for months about the invoices – it looked like a daunting task. Then I remembered this saying:

> **How do you eat an elephant? One bite at a time.**

I hired two new temporary staff members right away and broke this massive task into tiny daily steps. I wanted to make the goals reasonable so that we could celebrate a sense of achievement each day, so I used the SMART goal process:

Specific	What is a reasonable amount of money we agree we can collect each day if we stretch ourselves (our target)?
Measurable	How much money did we receive today?
Action orientated	How many calls do we need to make each day to get our target amount of money in?
Realistic	Can we realistically make that many calls in a day?
Timely	What are our daily, weekly, and monthly collection goals?

We made a chart showing our goals, put it on the wall, and then all got on the phone and started talking to customers.

It worked. The money started flowing in and we had something to celebrate every day – it was inspiring.

These are some of the things we celebrated while we worked hard to get back all the outstanding money from customers. You can adapt them to celebrate in your own environment.

Daily wins:

- A round of applause for the person with the largest amount of money received today.

- Congratulations at the end of the day for the person who had the most 'promises to pay' from customers.

- Congratulations for the person who gained commitment to pay for a very large payment, written up on the wall in the office and celebrated again when it arrived.

Weekly wins:

- Cakes for morning or afternoon coffee and tea breaks (sometimes a cake or biscuits a team member had made in celebration of their own personal win).

- On Monday or Tuesday, a cake specially decorated to show the results for the previous week.

- Drinks on a Friday afternoon if we'd already collected the team target in cash for that week.

Monthly wins:

- A special lunch out on the first Friday of the month if we'd collected the team target for the previous month.

- A department store voucher for the person who had collected the most money last month.

- A voucher for dinner out for two people for the person who had the smallest percentage of overdue accounts over 60 days old.

The first customers we tackled were those that had the largest amounts outstanding. Generally, they were large organisations. When we talked to them, we discussed all the invoices, not just those that were overdue. This is when I learnt to solve queries and problems super-fast, because so many invoices hadn't been paid because they had an error on them.

> **49% of invoices are not paid because of an error on the invoice.**

The sooner a problem was solved, the sooner a customer could pay. We solved problems when the customer was on the phone if we could. Step by step and, after almost a year, we had collected all of the 120-plus overdue amounts.

The company had over £3 million more in the bank than they had 12 months ago.

£ millions over 120 days old

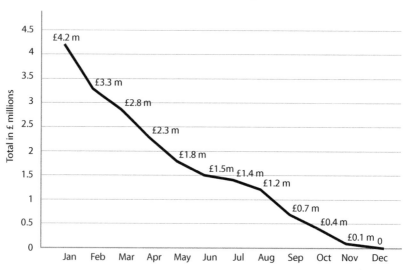

It was a massive cause for celebration and the Managing Director congratulated all of us in front of all the staff in the business.

LET'S CELEBRATE OUR WINS!

KEY POINTS

- Getting invoices paid on time can be made into a fun exercise with lots of milestones to achieve and celebrate and lots of rewarding relationships to develop.

- 'If it's going to be, it's up to me.' (Is it *you* that needs to take action?)

- 'If it has to be done – it might as well be fun.' (Did I make that up?)

- Break large tasks into small pieces to make it easier.

TO DO

1   Set your daily, weekly and monthly SMART collection goals.

2   Write your SMART goals and rewards up somewhere where you can see them all the time.

3   Decide on your daily, weekly and monthly rewards.

4   Celebrate all your wins!

CONCLUSION

I sincerely hope that my book has given you some insights into how I managed to make my business into a valuable company that someone wanted to buy because it had strong cashflow and great profits, and it really all stemmed from me working out this five-step solution to getting our invoices paid on time.

If you follow this five-step system your invoices will get paid too. Just think about the sales process a little differently and put into place a few administrative tasks, delivered with great customer service, in a non-confrontational environment:

- **Set up for success** just by checking a few facts.

- Send 100% **perfect invoices** that won't get delayed for payment because you are sorting out errors.

- Use the '**insider secret**' to further enhance your customer service superhero status.

- Feel **totally confident** in all your interactions with your customer.

- Know exactly the **right thing to say at the right time to the right person** to keep control of your invoices.

- **Be aware of potential bad debts** and know what to do to recoup your money.

- **Keep track of *all your money all the time*** – after all, it is your money.

As you follow the five steps in this book, the frustration, worry and angst you've experienced trying to get your invoices paid in the past will disappear.

Customers will start to pay you earlier, you'll begin to develop stronger relationships with customers, they'll get to like you, pay you, reorder and refer you to their business colleagues, leaving you free from worry about cashflow and free to focus on growing your profits and business value – and after all, isn't that why you started your business?

PEOPLE WE LIKE GET PAID FIRST

If people like you they pay you

IMPLEMENTATION

I hope you enjoyed my book and found it helpful.

If you did, gift copies of the book to your customers to help them get paid – so they can pay you sooner.

Order online or contact me for large orders.

If you would like help with any of the elements included in the book, or you would like to discuss an aspect of your receivables, please email me at jan@janreeves.com or contact me via my website https://janreeves.com/contact-jan/. I'll be happy to discuss how I can help further.

To your success getting paid!

Jan Reeves